Certification Study Companion Series

The Apress Certification Study Companion Series offers guidance and hands-on practice to support technical and business professionals who are studying for an exam in the pursuit of an industry certification. Professionals worldwide seek to achieve certifications in order to advance in a career role, reinforce knowledge in a specific discipline, or to apply for or change jobs. This series focuses on the most widely taken certification exams in a given field. It is designed to be user friendly, tracking to topics as they appear in a given exam and work alongside other certification material as professionals prepare for their exam.

More information about this series at `https://link.springer.com/bookseries/17100`.

Microsoft Certified: AI Transformation Leader Study Companion

Preparation for Exam AB-731

Kasam Shaikh

Apress®

Microsoft Certified: AI Transformation Leader Study Companion: Preparation for Exam AB-731

Kasam Shaikh
Near Patri Pool
Raheja Complex
Kalyan, Maharashtra, India

ISBN-13 (pbk): 979-8-8688-3167-6 ISBN-13 (electronic): 979-8-8688-3168-3
https://doi.org/10.1007/979-8-8688-3168-3

Managing Director, Apress Media LLC: Welmoed Spahr
Acquisitions Editor: Smriti Srivastava
Editorial Project Manager: Marina Engler

Cover designed by eStudioCalamar

Distributed to the book trade worldwide by Springer Science+Business Media New York, 1 New York Plaza, New York, NY 10004. Phone 1-800-SPRINGER, fax (201) 348-4505, e-mail orders-ny@springer-sbm.com, or visit www.springeronline.com. Apress Media, LLC is a Delaware LLC and the sole member (owner) is Springer Science + Business Media Finance Inc (SSBM Finance Inc). SSBM Finance Inc is a **Delaware** corporation.

For information on translations, please e-mail booktranslations@springernature.com; for reprint, paperback, or audio rights, please e-mail bookpermissions@springernature.com.

Apress titles may be purchased in bulk for academic, corporate, or promotional use. eBook versions and licenses are also available for most titles. For more information, reference our Print and eBook Bulk Sales web page at http://www.apress.com/bulk-sales.

Any source code or other supplementary material referenced by the author in this book is available to readers on GitHub. For more detailed information, please visit https://www.apress.com/gp/services/source-code.

If disposing of this product, please recycle the paper

This book is dedicated to my father—the late Mr. Ahmed Kasam Shaikh, who has always been a source of inspiration for me—and to my mentor, Mr. Sabarinath Iyer.

Table of Contents

About the Author

Kasam Shaikh is a four-time recipient of the prestigious Microsoft Most Valuable Professional (MVP) Award in AI—and the first and only Indian professional under the age of 40 to earn this honor consecutively for three years. A recognized global AI speaker, published author, and tech influencer, Kasam is widely known for his contributions to the AI ecosystem through his YouTube channel, mentoring initiatives, and thought leadership. He currently serves as an Enterprise Solutions Architect, driving AI transformation and AI adoption across business units. As the founder of Dear Azure - Azure INDIA, the largest Azure AI community in the region, he plays a key role in nurturing AI talent and fostering innovation. Additionally, he is acknowledged as a career expert in AI by RediffGuru and leads the AskBhai.AI Community.

About the Technical Reviewer

Rahat Yasir is a 12-time Microsoft AI MVP and one of Canada's Top 30 Software Developers Under 30 (2018). Over a career spanning USask's P2IRC, Immersive Design Studios, Intact Financial, OSEDEA, ISAAC Instruments, and IATA, he has built deep expertise in AI, data, and large-scale enterprise systems. He currently serves as Head of Data & AI Delivery at CAE, where he leads frontier AI-driven modernization across the company's factory of the future, civil aviation, and military domains. His work has earned the AI100 Early Adopters Award, the DataIQ Data & AI for Good Hero Organisation Award, and the DataIQ North America Grand Prix (2025).

Acknowledgments

I would first like to thank Almighty ALLAH, my mother Tahera, my better half Ruksar, and especially my daughter Maryam for motivating me throughout the writing process. I am highly thankful to Apress for considering me for this opportunity and for believing in me.

Disclaimer

This book represents the author's independent interpretation and understanding of AI transformation leadership concepts, enterprise AI adoption patterns, and the objectives of Exam AB-731 at the time of writing.

The views, explanations, examples, and recommendations presented throughout this book are based on professional experience, industry observations, and publicly available information. They do not represent official guidance, positions, or endorsements from Microsoft Corporation.

Microsoft Azure, Microsoft 365 Copilot, Copilot Studio, Microsoft Foundry, and related product names are trademarks of Microsoft Corporation.

As AI technologies, certification objectives, and Microsoft services continue to evolve rapidly, readers are strongly encouraged to refer to the official Microsoft Learn documentation and certification pages for the latest updates related to Exam AB-731 and associated technologies.

This book is intended as a practical learning and preparation guide, not as an official certification reference.

CHAPTER 1

The AI Transformation Leader and the AB-731 Exam

Introduction and Purpose of Exam AB-731

Artificial Intelligence has entered a phase where it is no longer treated as an isolated innovation initiative. It has become a boardroom conversation, a budget line item, and, increasingly, a competitive differentiator. What is changing is not only the capability of AI, but the expectation placed on organizations to use it responsibly and at scale. Leaders today are expected to take positions on AI—where to invest, where to avoid, how fast to move, and how to ensure that value is realized without introducing unacceptable risk.

In many conversations I've had with enterprise leaders, the challenge is rarely whether AI is powerful enough. The real question is whether organizations are prepared to use it responsibly, sustainably, and in ways that create measurable impact beyond initial excitement.

This is the context in which Microsoft introduced the **AI Transformation Leader certification (AB-731)**.

K. Shaikh, *Microsoft Certified: AI Transformation Leader Study Companion*, Certification Study Companion Series, https://doi.org/10.1007/979-8-8688-3168-3_1

Unlike earlier technology certifications that were designed for engineers or developers, AB-731 is deliberately positioned for decision-makers. It reflects a shift in how AI is being adopted across enterprises. The challenge is no longer limited to building models or deploying services. The real challenge lies in deciding *what should be built, why it should be built, and how it should be governed once deployed.*

The purpose of this exam is therefore not to validate technical expertise but to validate judgment. This distinction is central to understanding how the exam is structured and how it should be approached. As illustrated in Figure 1-1, the emphasis is on leadership thinking, identifying value, selecting the right approach, and ensuring responsible adoption rather than writing code or building systems.

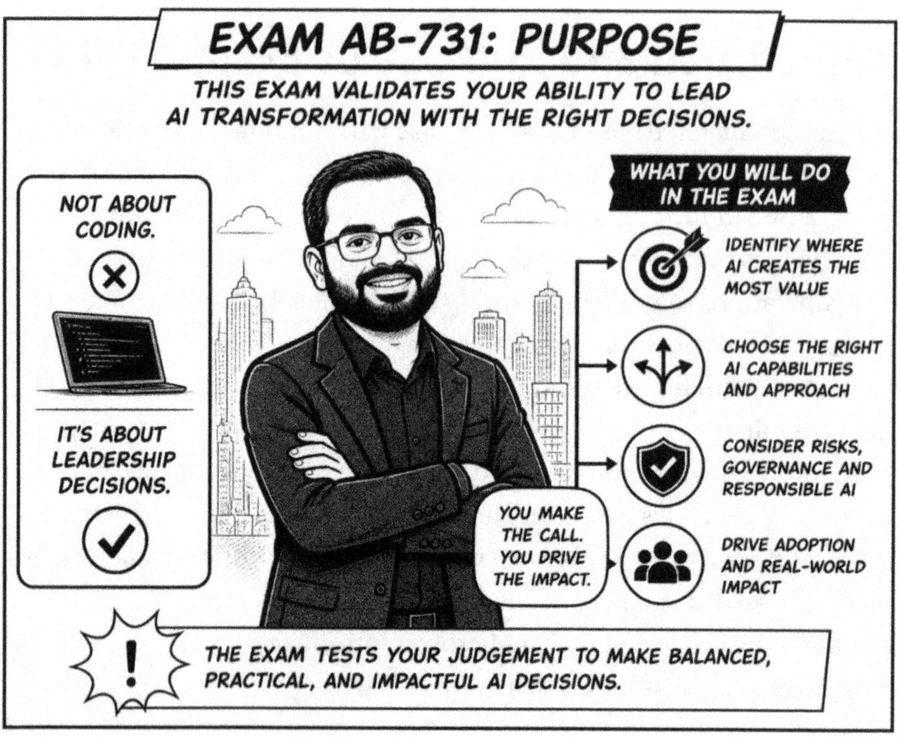

Figure 1-1. *Purpose of Exam AB-731: Leadership over Technical Execution*

Why a Certification for AI Transformation Leadership?

For many years, organizations approached AI through experimentation. Small teams explored use cases, prototypes were developed, and success was measured within limited boundaries. These efforts were valuable, but they rarely translated into enterprise-wide impact.

The emergence of generative AI has changed that dynamic significantly.

Capabilities that were once niche are now accessible through everyday tools. Employees can generate content, summarize information, and automate tasks with minimal effort. As a result, AI is no longer confined to technical teams. It is being introduced into functions such as finance, operations, marketing, and human resources.

This expansion introduces a different kind of complexity. Leaders must also evaluate the financial implications of AI initiatives. Some solutions may require significant upfront investment (Capital Expenditure or CapEx), while others operate on a consumption or subscription model (Operational Expenditure or OpEx). Beyond implementation costs, organizations are expected to consider the expected return on investment (ROI), ensuring that AI initiatives deliver measurable business outcomes rather than simply introducing new technology.

It is no longer enough to ask whether a model performs well. Leaders must now consider

- Whether the use of AI aligns with business objectives
- Whether the organization is ready to adopt it at scale
- Whether risks related to data, bias, or misuse are understood and managed
- Whether the solution will be trusted and used by employees

These are not technical questions. They are leadership questions.

The AB-731 exam exists to evaluate whether a candidate can navigate this complexity with clarity and responsibility.

Understanding the Scope of AB-731

The scope of AB-731 is intentionally broad, but not deep in a technical sense. It covers the full life cycle of AI decision-making from a leadership perspective, starting with identifying opportunities and extending to adoption, governance, and long-term impact.

At its core, the exam expects you to operate at three levels simultaneously.

First, you must be able to recognize where AI creates value. This requires an understanding of business processes and the ability to identify inefficiencies, bottlenecks, or opportunities for improvement. Not every problem requires AI, and one of the most important skills a leader can develop is knowing when *not* to use it.

Second, you must understand the landscape of available solutions. Microsoft's ecosystem includes offerings such as Microsoft 365 Copilot, Copilot Studio, and Azure AI services. Each of these serves a different purpose, and the exam tests your ability to select the right approach based on context rather than preference.

With the recent evolution of Microsoft's AI ecosystem, leaders are also expected to be aware of the positioning of **Azure AI Foundry** as part of the broader platform strategy. While deep technical knowledge is not required, understanding that enterprise AI solutions are increasingly built on integrated platforms rather than isolated services is important for making correct decisions in scenario-based questions.

Third, you must consider adoption and governance. This is where many AI initiatives struggle. A technically sound solution that is not trusted or not aligned with organizational workflows will fail to deliver value. Similarly, solutions introduced without proper governance can create risks that outweigh their benefits.

The scope of the exam brings these dimensions together. It is not testing isolated knowledge areas; it is testing how well you can balance them.

How AB-731 Differs from Traditional Certifications

To fully understand the purpose of this exam, it is useful to compare it with more traditional certifications.

In a typical technical exam, you are expected to know

- How a service works
- How to configure it
- How to troubleshoot it

The questions are often direct, and there is usually a clearly correct answer based on factual knowledge.

AB-731 takes a different approach.

Here, you are presented with a situation rather than a direct question. The scenario may involve business objectives, organizational constraints, and sometimes conflicting priorities. Multiple answers may appear correct at first glance. The challenge is to identify which option best aligns with the overall context.

This requires a different mindset.

Instead of asking, *"Do I know this feature?"*, you need to ask

- What is the organization trying to achieve?
- What are the risks involved?
- What is the simplest approach that delivers value?
- How will this be adopted and governed?

The correct answer is rarely the most advanced or technically impressive option. It is usually the one that is **practical, scalable, and aligned with business needs**.

A Leadership Lens on AI Decision-Making

To make sense of this, it helps to visualize how decisions are made at a leadership level.

Figure 1-2 illustrates a simple but powerful way to think about AI decisions in an enterprise context.

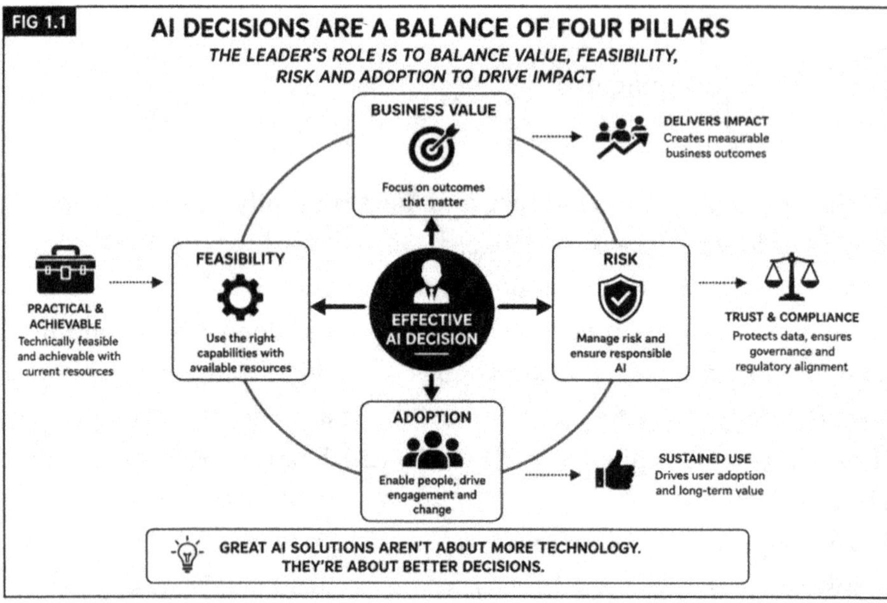

Figure 1-2. *AI Decision Framework for Leaders*

Figure 1-2 highlights that every AI decision sits at the intersection of four key considerations.

The first is value. If a solution does not create measurable impact, it should not be prioritized. The second is feasibility, which includes technical capability, data readiness, and organizational capacity.

The third is risk, covering aspects such as data privacy, bias, and compliance. The fourth is adoption, which determines whether the solution will actually be used in practice.

In many cases, organizations overemphasize one of these dimensions. For example, they may focus heavily on technical feasibility while ignoring adoption, or they may prioritize innovation without fully understanding risk. The result is imbalance, and that imbalance often leads to failure.

The AB-731 exam consistently rewards answers that demonstrate balance across these dimensions.

Setting the Right Mindset for the Exam

Preparing for this exam is not about memorizing definitions or learning tools in isolation. It is about developing a way of thinking.

You must begin to view AI not as a technology problem but as a business capability that must be introduced carefully and deliberately. This means recognizing that the "best" solution is not always the most advanced one. It is the one that fits the organization's context.

It also means accepting that trade-offs are inevitable. Increasing speed may increase risk. Adding flexibility may increase complexity. Improving control may reduce adoption. A transformation leader must navigate these trade-offs without losing sight of the overall objective.

This is exactly what the exam is designed to test.

AI is no longer seen purely as a technical domain. It is now recognized as a strategic capability that requires leadership oversight.

By focusing on decision-making, value creation, and responsible adoption, the exam aligns closely with how AI is being implemented in real organizations. It prepares candidates not just to pass an exam but to operate effectively in environments where AI decisions have meaningful business impact.

Skills Measured and Exam Weighting

If the previous section clarified *why* Exam AB-731 exists, this section focuses on *how it evaluates you*. Understanding the skills measured is not just about knowing the syllabus—it is about decoding how Microsoft expects a leader to think when making AI-related decisions.

At first glance, the exam structure appears straightforward. It is divided into three broad domains, each carrying a specific weight. However, approaching these domains as isolated topics would be a mistake. The real intent of the exam is not to test each area independently but to assess how well you can **connect them in a real-world scenario**.

How to Read the Exam Structure

The official breakdown of the exam typically reflects three core areas:

- Identifying the business value of generative AI
- Understanding AI capabilities and solution options
- Planning adoption, governance, and responsible AI

Each of these carries a percentage weight, indicating its relative importance. However, the weight should not be interpreted as a simple distribution of questions. In practice, most questions span across multiple domains.

For example, a single question might describe a business scenario where

- There is a clear need for productivity improvement
- Multiple AI solutions are available
- There are concerns around data security and governance

To answer such a question correctly, you need to

- Recognize the **business value**
- Choose the **right capability**
- Consider **risk and adoption**

This is why understanding the **interplay between domains** is far more important than memorizing them individually.

Domain 1: Identifying Business Value of Generative AI

This domain typically carries the highest or near-highest weight, and for good reason. It reflects the starting point of any AI initiative: identifying where value exists.

From an exam perspective, this is where many candidates underestimate the complexity. The expectation is not to identify obvious use cases but to distinguish between

- What is *technically possible*
- What is *practically valuable*

In real organizations, these two are often very different.

You may encounter scenarios where AI can be applied, but the expected return is unclear or marginal. In such cases, the correct decision is often to avoid overinvestment. The exam tests your ability to prioritize—not just to recognize possibilities.

Another important aspect here is understanding the difference between

- Productivity gains (doing the same work faster)
- Transformation outcomes (changing how work is done)

Leaders must recognize when a simple productivity improvement is sufficient, and when a deeper transformation is justified. The exam frequently explores this distinction.

Domain 2: Understanding AI Capabilities and Solution Options

The second domain focuses on your ability to select the right solution based on context. This includes familiarity with Microsoft's AI offerings, but only at a conceptual level.

You are expected to understand

- Where Microsoft 365 Copilot fits
- When to use Copilot Studio
- When Azure AI services are more appropriate

Recent updates in Microsoft's ecosystem emphasize the role of **Azure AI Foundry** as a unified platform for building and managing AI solutions. While the exam does not expect deep technical knowledge, it increasingly reflects a shift toward platform-based thinking rather than isolated service selection.

The challenge in this domain is not remembering features but making **comparative decisions**.

For instance, you may be presented with a scenario where

- A solution needs to be deployed quickly
- Users are already working within Microsoft 365
- There is limited technical expertise available

In such a case, a solution like Microsoft 365 Copilot is likely more appropriate than building a custom application on Azure.

On the other hand, if the requirement involves

- Custom workflows
- Integration with proprietary systems
- Advanced control over data and models

then Azure AI services may be a better fit.

The exam tests your ability to recognize these nuances and choose accordingly.

Domain 3: Adoption, Governance, and Responsible AI

This domain often carries slightly less weight numerically, but it is critical in determining the correct answer in many questions.

In practice, this is where leadership maturity becomes most visible.

AI solutions do not fail because they cannot be built. They fail because they are not adopted, not trusted, or not governed properly. The exam reflects this reality by introducing scenarios where

- Data privacy is a concern
- Outputs may be unreliable
- Users may resist adoption

Your role is to identify approaches that address these concerns proactively.

This includes

- Ensuring transparency in how AI is used
- Establishing clear usage policies
- Managing risks such as bias and hallucinations
- Aligning solutions with organizational compliance requirements

The key insight here is that governance is not an afterthought. It is part of the decision-making process from the beginning.

How the Weighting Should Influence Your Preparation

It is tempting to allocate your study time strictly based on percentage weight. While this may help in covering the syllabus, it does not fully prepare you for the exam.

A more effective approach is to recognize that

- **Business value drives the decision**
- **Capabilities enable the decision**
- **Governance validates the decision**

These are not separate steps; they are part of a single thought process. In many questions, the correct answer is the one that

- Delivers clear business value
- Uses an appropriate and not overly complex solution
- Addresses risk and adoption concerns

If any one of these elements is missing, the answer is unlikely to be correct.

Visualizing the Exam Domains Together

To better understand how these domains interact, it is useful to view them as a connected system rather than independent areas. A solution that delivers value but ignores governance introduces risk. If it is technically sound but not adopted, it fails to create impact.

As illustrated in Figure 1-3, effective AI decisions emerge only when value, capability, and responsibility are aligned.

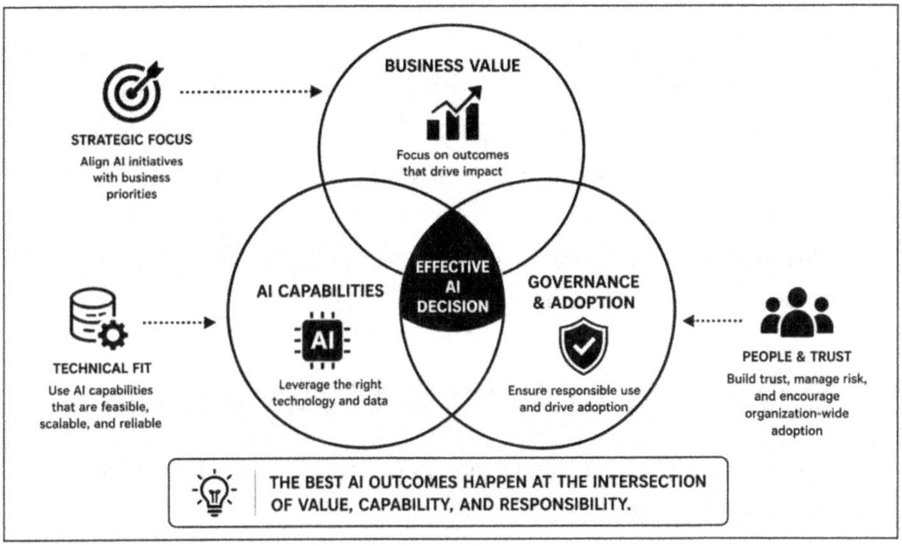

Figure 1-3. *Three Dimensions of Effective AI Decisions: Value, Capability, and Responsibility in Balance*

This relationship becomes clearer when viewed as an intersection rather than separate concerns, where the most effective AI decisions emerge only when value, capability, and responsibility are aligned together. The exam is designed to test your ability to operate in this intersection.

Common Misinterpretations of the Exam Weighting

There are a few patterns that frequently lead to incorrect answers.

One common mistake is overemphasizing technology. Candidates often choose answers that appear more advanced or comprehensive, assuming they are better. In many cases, the simpler option is more aligned with the scenario.

Another mistake is ignoring implicit constraints. Questions often include subtle hints about organizational limitations—such as lack of expertise, strict compliance requirements, or the need for rapid deployment. These signals are critical in choosing the right answer.

A third mistake is treating governance as secondary. In this exam, governance is often the deciding factor between two otherwise valid options.

A Practical Way to Approach Every Question

By now, a pattern should be clear. Every question can be approached by mentally evaluating three things:

- What value is expected?
- What solution best fits the context?
- What risks or adoption challenges must be addressed?

You do not need to formalize this as a checklist during the exam, but developing this habit during preparation will significantly improve your accuracy.

The skills measured in AB-731 are not theoretical constructs. They reflect the real challenges faced by leaders implementing AI in organizations today. The weighting provides guidance, but the real test lies in your ability to integrate these domains into a single, coherent decision-making approach.

The AI Transformation Leader vs. Technical AI Roles

As organizations accelerate their adoption of artificial intelligence, a subtle but important confusion often emerges. Many assume that leading AI initiatives requires deep technical expertise. While technical knowledge is valuable, it is not the defining characteristic of an AI Transformation Leader. The role operates at a different level—one that is closer to decision-making than implementation.

To understand this clearly, it is useful to step back and observe how AI initiatives actually unfold within an enterprise.

In most organizations, AI efforts involve multiple roles working together. Data scientists design models, engineers build systems, and architects ensure that solutions are scalable and secure. These roles are essential. However, they are not responsible for deciding *why* a solution should exist in the first place or whether it aligns with business priorities. That responsibility lies with the transformation leader.

The distinction may appear subtle, but it has significant implications—both for how you approach the exam and how you approach AI in practice.

A Shift from Building to Deciding

Technical roles are naturally oriented toward execution. When presented with a problem, they focus on how it can be solved using available tools and techniques. Their success is measured by the quality, performance, and reliability of the solution they build.

An AI Transformation Leader operates differently. The focus is not on building the best possible solution but on ensuring that the *right* solution is chosen.

This involves asking questions that are often overlooked in technically driven discussions:

- Is this problem worth solving with AI?
- What is the expected business outcome?
- Do we have the data required to support this?
- What risks are associated with this approach?
- How will this solution be adopted across the organization?

These questions are not technical in nature, but they determine the success or failure of the initiative.

In many real-world scenarios, technically strong solutions fail because these questions were not addressed early enough. The transformation leader's role is to ensure that they are.

Where the Roles Intersect and Where They Do Not

It is important to recognize that the AI Transformation Leader does not operate in isolation. The role depends on collaboration with technical teams. However, the nature of that collaboration is different.

Technical experts provide depth. They understand how systems work, what is possible, and what trade-offs exist at an implementation level. The transformation leader provides direction. They ensure that technical efforts are aligned with business goals and organizational constraints.

The transformation leader defines the *what* and *why*, while technical teams focus on the *how*. This distinction becomes clearer when viewed across roles, as illustrated in Figure 1-4.

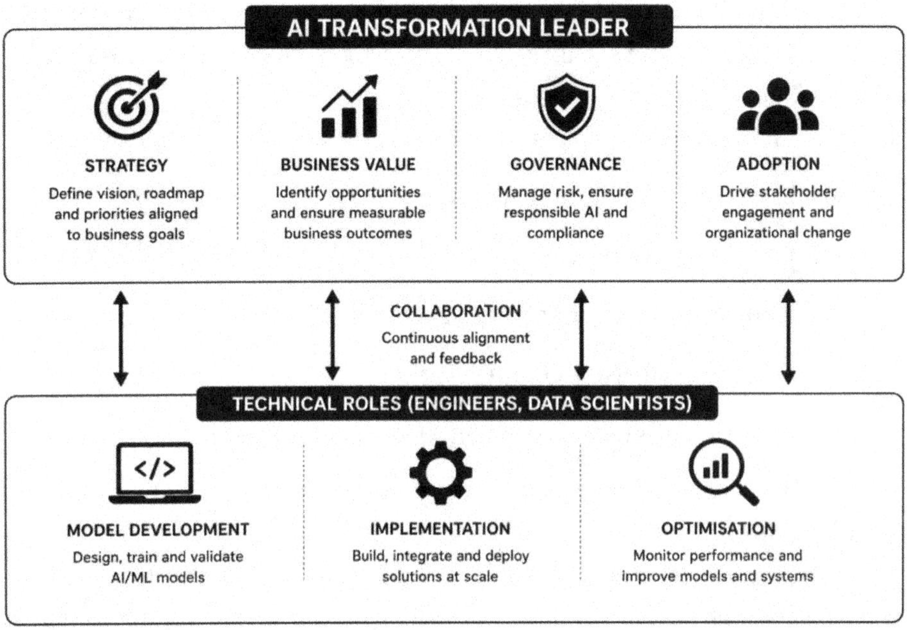

Figure 1-4. *AI Transformation Leader vs. Technical Roles—Direction vs. Execution*

Confusion arises when these boundaries are blurred. If leaders become too focused on technical detail, they risk losing sight of business outcomes. Conversely, if technical teams are expected to define strategy without proper context, solutions may become misaligned.

The exam is designed to reinforce this separation. It places you in the position of a leader who must guide decisions without getting drawn into implementation specifics.

Decision Ownership vs. Execution Ownership

Another way to understand this distinction is through ownership.

In an AI initiative, ownership is divided into two broad categories: decision ownership and execution ownership.

Execution ownership lies with technical teams. They are responsible for delivering a working solution. Their concerns include performance, scalability, accuracy, and integration.

Decision ownership lies with the transformation leader. This includes

- Selecting which initiatives to pursue
- Prioritizing use cases
- Determining acceptable levels of risk
- Defining governance frameworks
- Ensuring alignment with organizational strategy

The AB-731 exam consistently tests your ability to operate within this second category.

For example, you may encounter a scenario where multiple solutions are technically feasible. The correct answer is not the one that demonstrates the most advanced implementation but the one that reflects sound decision-making.

The Risk of Over-technical Thinking

One of the most common mistakes candidates make is over-indexing on technical thinking.

When presented with a scenario, it is natural to look for the most sophisticated or comprehensive solution. However, in a leadership context, sophistication does not always translate to effectiveness.

Consider a situation where an organization wants to improve internal communication and documentation processes. A technically driven approach might involve building a custom AI system with advanced capabilities. While this may be feasible, it introduces complexity, cost, and time.

A leadership-driven approach might instead consider whether existing tools such as Microsoft 365 Copilot can address the need more efficiently. Even if the solution is less customizable, it may deliver faster adoption and lower risk.

The exam frequently presents such trade-offs. In most enterprise situations, it is the one that balances value with practicality rather than maximizing technical capability.

Leadership Requires Context, Not Just Knowledge

Another important distinction is the role of context.

Technical expertise often focuses on universal principles, how models behave, how systems are designed, and how performance can be optimized. These principles are consistent across scenarios.

Leadership decisions, however, are highly context-dependent.

The same solution may be appropriate in one organization and unsuitable in another. Factors such as organizational culture, data maturity, regulatory environment, and workforce readiness all influence the decision.

This is why the exam places strong emphasis on scenario-based questions. It is not enough to know what a tool can do. You must understand when it should be used and when it should not.

Evolving Role of the AI Transformation Leader

As AI continues to evolve, so does the role of the transformation leader.

Initially, the focus may be on identifying opportunities and initiating pilots. Over time, the responsibility shifts toward scaling solutions, standardizing practices, and establishing governance frameworks.

With the increasing maturity of platforms such as Azure AI and the emergence of integrated environments like **Azure AI Foundry**, the role of the leader is also expanding to include platform-level decision-making. Leaders are expected to understand not just individual tools, but how these tools fit into a broader enterprise architecture.

This does not require deep technical knowledge, but it does require awareness of how different components interact and how decisions made at one level impact others.

A Practical Illustration

To make this more concrete, consider a scenario.

An organization wants to use AI to improve customer support. The technical team proposes building a custom chatbot using Azure AI services. At the same time, there is an option to use a pre-built solution with limited customization.

A technically driven decision might favor the custom solution, as it offers greater flexibility. A transformation leader, however, would consider additional factors:

- How quickly does the organization need results?
- Does the team have the expertise to maintain a custom solution?
- Are there compliance requirements that need to be addressed?
- Will users trust and adopt the solution?

The final decision may still favor the custom approach—but only if these questions are satisfactorily addressed.

This is the level of thinking the exam expects.

Understanding the distinction between an AI Transformation Leader and technical roles is fundamental to succeeding in AB-731.

The focus of the exam is not to test your ability to build solutions. It is testing your ability to guide decisions in complex, real-world environments. It rewards clarity, context awareness, and balanced judgment.

Common Reasons Enterprise AI Initiatives Fail

There is a common perception that AI initiatives fail because the technology is not mature enough. In practice, the opposite is often true. The technology has advanced rapidly, but organizations struggle to extract consistent value from it. The gap is not technical; it is strategic and organizational.

Understanding why AI initiatives fail is not just an academic exercise. It is central to how you should approach the AB-731 exam. Many of the scenarios you will encounter are designed around these failure patterns. The correct answer is often the one that avoids a mistake that organizations repeatedly make in real life.

To appreciate this fully, it is useful to examine how AI initiatives typically unfold.

The Illusion of a Strong Start

Most AI initiatives begin with optimism. There is executive interest, funding is allocated, and teams are formed. Early demonstrations often show promising results. Prototypes work, and stakeholders begin to see potential.

At this stage, everything appears to be moving in the right direction.

However, this early momentum can be misleading. Prototypes are built under controlled conditions. Data is curated, use cases are narrow, and success criteria are often loosely defined. Moving from this stage to enterprise-wide adoption introduces a completely different level of complexity.

This is where many initiatives begin to struggle.

Failure Begins with Misaligned Objectives

One of the most common issues is the absence of a clearly defined business objective.

Organizations sometimes adopt AI because it is seen as a strategic necessity rather than a targeted solution. Teams are encouraged to "explore AI opportunities," but without clear direction, these efforts become fragmented.

The result is a collection of experiments rather than a cohesive strategy.

In such situations, even technically successful solutions fail to deliver impact. There is no clear metric for success, no alignment with business priorities, and no path to scaling.

From an exam perspective, scenarios like this often require you to recognize that the problem is not the solution; it is the lack of clarity in the objective.

Overengineering Too Early

Another recurring pattern is the tendency to overengineer solutions at an early stage.

Technical teams, driven by capability, may design highly sophisticated systems with multiple integrations, custom models, and complex workflows. While these solutions may be impressive, they introduce significant challenges:

- Longer development cycles
- Increased cost
- Higher maintenance overhead
- Greater difficulty in adoption

In many cases, a simpler approach could have delivered comparable value with far less effort. I have seen organizations spend months designing highly customized AI solutions, only to realize later that a simpler approach could have solved the immediate business problem far faster. In many enterprise environments, speed of adoption often creates more value than technical sophistication alone.

This is particularly relevant in the context of modern AI tools. Solutions like Microsoft 365 Copilot are designed to provide immediate value within existing workflows. Choosing a complex custom solution when a simpler option exists is a common mistake, and one that the exam frequently tests.

Data Readiness Is Often Assumed, Not Validated

AI systems are only as effective as the data they rely on. Despite this, data readiness is often treated as an afterthought.

Organizations may assume that because data exists, it is usable. In reality, data may be

- Incomplete
- Inconsistent
- Poorly structured
- Difficult to access due to security or compliance constraints

These issues become more pronounced when scaling AI solutions. What works in a controlled prototype environment may fail when exposed to real-world data conditions.

In many organizations, these challenges are further compounded by legacy systems that were never designed to support modern AI capabilities. Important business information may reside across multiple applications with inconsistent formats and varying levels of accessibility. Before investing in AI, leaders should evaluate not only the quality of available data but also whether existing systems can provide reliable and secure access to that information.

Leaders must recognize that data readiness is not just a technical concern. It is a foundational requirement that influences feasibility, risk, and ultimately, value.

The Adoption Gap

Perhaps the most underestimated factor in AI success is user adoption.

A solution can be technically sound, well-integrated, and aligned with business objectives and still fail if users do not trust or understand it.

This lack of adoption can stem from several factors:

- Lack of transparency in how the AI works
- Concerns about accuracy or reliability
- Fear of job displacement
- Insufficient training or change management

In many organizations, adoption is treated as a final step rather than an integral part of the design process. By the time these issues are addressed, momentum has already been lost.

The AB-731 exam places significant emphasis on this dimension. Answers that consider adoption alongside technical feasibility are consistently favored.

Governance As an Afterthought

As AI systems become more integrated into business processes, the risks associated with them increase. These risks include

- Exposure of sensitive data
- Biased or misleading outputs
- Misuse of AI-generated content

Despite this, governance is often introduced late in the life cycle, once solutions are already in use. This reactive approach creates gaps that are difficult to close.

Effective governance requires

- Clear policies on usage
- Defined accountability
- Monitoring and oversight mechanisms

Leaders must ensure that governance is embedded from the beginning, not layered on afterward.

Fragmentation Across the Organization

In many enterprises, AI initiatives are not coordinated. Different departments pursue their own use cases, often using different tools and approaches.

While this may accelerate experimentation, it creates challenges in the long term:

- Inconsistent standards
- Duplication of effort
- Difficulty in scaling solutions
- Increased risk exposure

A transformation leader must bring coherence to these efforts. This does not mean centralizing everything, but it does mean establishing shared principles and frameworks.

Visualizing the Failure Patterns

To better understand how these issues are connected, consider the life cycle of an AI initiative.

Common Failure Points in AI Initiatives

Failure in AI initiatives does not occur at a single point. It can emerge at any stage, depending on where alignment breaks down. At the idea stage, lack of clarity leads to weak direction. During the pilot stage, overengineering introduces complexity. At the scaling stage, data issues become visible. Finally, at the adoption stage, lack of trust and governance prevents sustained use.

The role of the transformation leader is to anticipate these points of failure and address them proactively. This becomes easier to understand when viewed across the life cycle of an AI initiative, as illustrated in Figure 1-5.

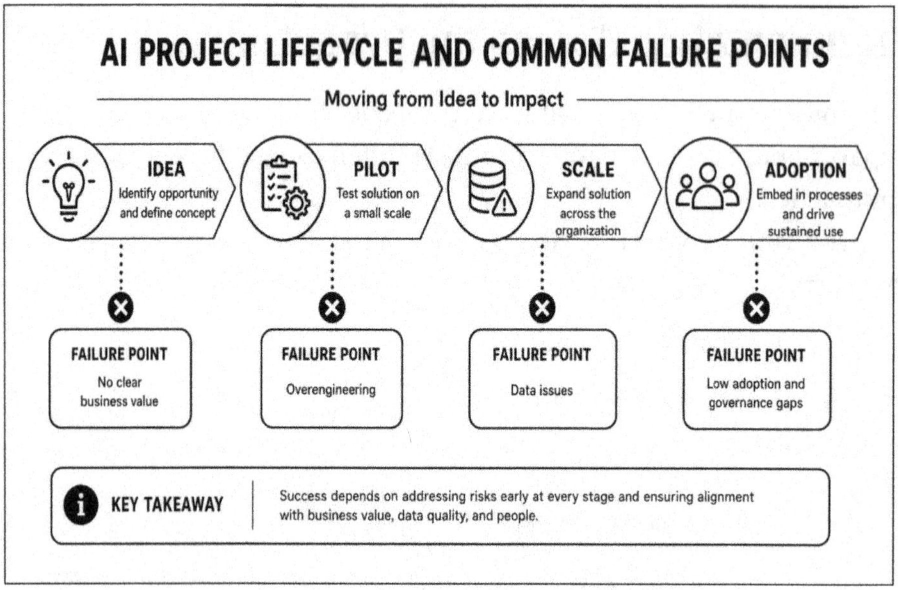

Figure 1-5. *AI Initiative Life Cycle and Common Failure Points: From Idea to Adoption*

A Pattern the Exam Consistently Reflects

If there is one consistent theme across AB-731, it is this: the best answer is rarely the most technically advanced one.

Instead, what matters most in these scenarios is the one that

- Aligns clearly with business value
- Avoids unnecessary complexity
- Considers data and feasibility
- Addresses adoption and governance

In many questions, two options may appear equally valid from a technical standpoint. The differentiator is often how well they account for these broader considerations.

AI initiatives do not fail because organizations lack tools. In one BFSI program I reviewed, a perfectly engineered fraud detection model was never deployed, not because it failed technically, but because compliance teams could not audit its decisions.

This is precisely why the role of the AI Transformation Leader is critical.

By understanding these failure patterns, you are not only preparing for the exam, you are developing the ability to recognize and avoid the same mistakes in real-world scenarios.

Now let's shift toward how to approach scenario-based exam questions. This will bring together everything discussed so far and provide a practical way to apply it during the exam.

How to Approach Scenario-Based Exam Questions

By this point, you have seen how the exam is structured, what skills are measured, and why many AI initiatives fail in practice. The next step is to translate that understanding into a practical approach for answering questions.

This is where many candidates struggle—not because they lack knowledge, but because they approach the exam in the wrong way.

AB-731 is not a recall-based exam. It does not reward memorization of definitions or features. Instead, it presents you with situations that resemble real-world decision-making. These scenarios are often layered, with multiple factors influencing the final answer.

The challenge is not to identify what is possible, but to determine what is most appropriate.

Understanding the Nature of Scenario-Based Questions

A typical question in this exam will not directly ask you about a tool or concept. Instead, it will describe a situation involving an organization, a business objective, and a set of constraints.

These scenarios are intentionally written to mirror real-world ambiguity. Information may be incomplete, priorities may not be explicitly stated, and more than one option may appear correct.

This is deliberate.

In practice, leaders rarely operate with perfect information. Decisions must be made based on context, signals, and judgment. The exam replicates this environment.

To navigate this effectively, you need a structured way of thinking—one that allows you to interpret the scenario before evaluating the options.

Step 1: Identify the True Objective

Every scenario begins with an objective, but it is not always stated directly.

Sometimes the objective is explicit, such as improving productivity or reducing operational cost. In other cases, it is implied through the description of the situation.

The key is to look beyond surface-level details and identify what the organization is ultimately trying to achieve.

For example, a scenario may describe a company struggling with slow document processing. The immediate issue appears operational, but the underlying objective is likely efficiency and turnaround time.

If you misinterpret the objective, even the most logical answer will be incorrect.

Step 2: Recognize Constraints and Signals

Once the objective is clear, the next step is to identify constraints.

These are often embedded within the scenario and may include

- Security or compliance requirements
- Limited technical expertise
- Budget or time constraints
- Existing tools and environments

Constraints are critical because they shape what is feasible.

For instance, if a scenario emphasizes strict data governance, an approach that involves extensive customization without clear controls is unlikely to be appropriate. Similarly, if rapid deployment is a priority, solutions that require significant development effort may not be suitable.

These signals are rarely highlighted explicitly. You must learn to recognize them through careful reading.

Financial considerations are another important constraint. Organizations may already have investments in Microsoft technologies, budget limitations, or expectations around demonstrating business value. In many scenarios, the most appropriate solution is not necessarily the most feature-rich but the one that delivers the required outcome in a cost-effective and sustainable manner.

Step 3: Evaluate the Level of Complexity

A common trap in this exam is overestimating what is required.

When presented with multiple options, candidates often gravitate toward the most comprehensive or technically advanced solution. This instinct is understandable, especially for those with a technical background.

However, in a leadership context, complexity must be justified.

If a simpler solution can achieve the objective with lower risk and faster adoption, it is often the better choice. Introducing unnecessary complexity increases cost, delays implementation, and creates barriers to adoption.

The exam frequently tests this judgment. The correct answer is not the one that demonstrates maximum capability but the one that demonstrates appropriate capability.

Step 4: Consider Adoption and Governance Together

One of the defining characteristics of AB-731 is the emphasis on adoption and governance.

These are not separate considerations; they are interconnected.

A solution that is easy to deploy but difficult to govern introduces risk. Conversely, a solution that is highly controlled but difficult to use may fail due to lack of adoption.

The correct answer is typically the one that balances both.

For example, if a scenario involves introducing AI into daily workflows, the solution must not only be technically sound but also intuitive for users. At the same time, it must operate within defined governance boundaries to ensure responsible use.

Ignoring either dimension leads to an incomplete decision.

A Practical Decision Flow

To bring these steps together, it helps to visualize the decision process as a flow.

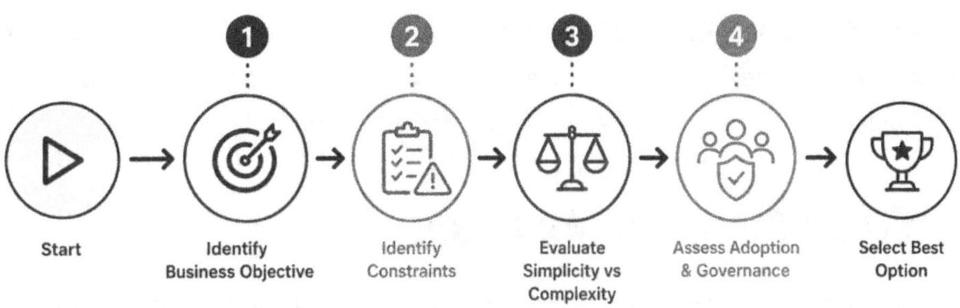

Figure 1-6. *Decision Flow for Evaluating Scenario-Based Questions*

Figure 1-6 represents a structured way of thinking through each question. The process begins with understanding the objective. Without this, all subsequent steps are misaligned. Constraints are then identified to narrow down feasible options. Complexity is evaluated to avoid overengineering. Finally, adoption and governance are considered before selecting the answer.

This flow is not something you need to consciously map out during the exam. With practice, it becomes intuitive.

Recognizing Patterns in Answer Choices

Another important aspect of the exam is recognizing how answer choices are constructed.

Typically, options fall into certain patterns:

- One option is overly complex and not aligned with the scenario.
- One option ignores key constraints.
- One option appears reasonable but lacks consideration for governance or adoption.
- One option balances all relevant factors.

In practice, organizations tend to favor the one that demonstrates balance.

This does not mean it is always the simplest option, but it is rarely the most extreme one. Extreme answers—those that prioritize one dimension at the expense of others—are often incorrect.

Avoiding Common Mistakes

Even with a clear approach, certain mistakes are easy to make.

One is focusing too heavily on familiar tools. If you have experience with a particular technology, you may be inclined to choose it even when it is not the best fit for the scenario. The exam expects neutrality; decisions should be driven by context, not preference.

Another mistake is ignoring subtle cues. Words such as "quickly," "securely," or "with minimal effort" are not incidental. They indicate priorities that should influence your decision.

A third mistake is assuming that more control is always better. While governance is important, excessive control can hinder adoption. The correct answer often strikes a balance.

Building Confidence Through Practice

Like any skill, this approach improves with practice.

As you work through questions, focus not only on whether your answer is correct, but also on why it is correct. Try to identify which factor—value, feasibility, risk, or adoption—was most influential in the decision.

Over time, patterns will emerge. You will begin to anticipate the intent behind questions and recognize the types of answers that align with that intent.

Approaching scenario-based questions effectively is less about technique and more about mindset.

The exam is designed to simulate real-world decision-making, where clarity is often more valuable than complexity. By focusing on objectives, constraints, and balance, you position yourself to make decisions that are both practical and aligned with organizational needs.

This section brings together the key themes of the chapter. You have seen how the exam is structured, what it tests, why initiatives fail, and how to approach decisions.

Summary

This chapter set the foundation for understanding both the intent of Exam AB-731 and the mindset required to approach it effectively. Rather than introducing AI as a purely technical subject, it positioned AI as a leadership responsibility, one that requires clarity of thought, balanced decision-making, and an awareness of organizational realities.

Taken together, this chapter is not about memorizing concepts. It is about developing a way of thinking. Success in AB-731 depends on your ability to view AI through a leadership lens, where decisions are shaped by context, trade-offs are inevitable, and the goal is not perfection but alignment. This shift in thinking is captured in Figure 1-7.

Figure 1-7. *AI Leadership Mindset: From Understanding to Application*

As you move into the next chapter, this mindset becomes even more important. The discussion will shift toward generative AI and its role in creating business value, but the underlying principle remains the same: understanding technology is useful, but knowing when and how to apply it is what truly defines an AI Transformation Leader.

CHAPTER 2

Generative AI Fundamentals for Business Value

Introduction

Generative AI has rapidly transformed from a technology trend into a business priority. Organizations across industries are now exploring how AI can improve productivity, accelerate decision-making, enhance customer experiences, and create new operational capabilities. Unlike earlier forms of AI that often remained confined to specialized systems, generative AI became immediately accessible to everyday users through natural language interactions and AI-assisted workflows.

This shift has changed the expectations placed on business leaders. A few years ago, many executive discussions around AI were still exploratory. Today, the conversation has become far more practical. Leaders are now expected to identify where generative AI creates measurable value, where risks emerge, and how adoption can scale responsibly across the organization.

This chapter examines generative AI from a leadership and business perspective. It explores how generative AI differs from traditional AI, where organizations are currently seeing measurable value, and how

K. Shaikh, *Microsoft Certified: AI Transformation Leader Study Companion*, Certification Study Companion Series, https://doi.org/10.1007/979-8-8688-3168-3_2

leaders should think about productivity gains, innovation outcomes, cost considerations, and return on investment. Most importantly, the chapter focuses on developing the judgment required to identify practical, high-value AI opportunities in real-world enterprise environments.

What Generative AI Is (Leader Perspective)

For many business leaders, generative AI initially appears almost magical. A user types a question into a chat interface, and within seconds the system produces a detailed response, creates an image, summarizes a report, generates code, or drafts a presentation. The speed and fluency of these interactions often create the impression that the technology possesses deep understanding or reasoning capabilities comparable to human intelligence.

In reality, generative AI should be understood less as a form of human-like intelligence and more as an advanced pattern-generation system trained on extremely large volumes of data.

From a leadership perspective, however, the technical mechanics are not the most important aspect. What matters more is understanding why this technology is influencing enterprise operations so rapidly and where its practical business value originates.

At its core, generative AI refers to AI systems capable of producing new content based on instructions, context, or examples provided by users. Unlike earlier systems designed mainly to classify information or automate predefined workflows, generative AI creates outputs dynamically. These outputs may include

- Text
- Summaries
- Software code
- Images

- Recommendations
- Conversational responses
- Knowledge-based assistance

This distinction between analyzing information and generating new content is what makes generative AI fundamentally different from many earlier enterprise technologies.

For decades, most enterprise systems focused on structured processes. Employees interacted with predefined screens, workflows, and rule-based systems. Generative AI changes this interaction model significantly because employees can now communicate with systems conversationally using natural language.

This reduces technical friction.

An employee no longer needs to understand complex query structures or specialized software navigation to extract value from technology. Instead, they describe intent in plain language. The AI system interprets that intent and attempts to generate an appropriate response.

That accessibility changed adoption patterns almost overnight. Earlier AI systems often remained invisible to most employees, but generative AI quickly became part of everyday work.

In many organizations, earlier AI systems were visible only to technical teams or analysts. Generative AI became accessible to almost everyone immediately. Marketing teams could generate content drafts. HR teams could summarize policy documents. Developers could receive coding assistance. Customer service teams could draft responses automatically. Executives could generate meeting summaries or strategic outlines within seconds.

This broad accessibility transformed AI from a specialized capability into a workforce-level capability.

However, accessibility should not be confused with simplicity.

One of the biggest misunderstandings surrounding generative AI is the assumption that because the interface feels simple, the organizational implications are also simple. In practice, generative AI introduces complex questions around trust, governance, accuracy, compliance, and workforce adoption.

For example, an AI-generated summary may appear highly convincing while still containing inaccuracies or omissions. A generated customer response may sound professional while unintentionally introducing compliance concerns. A coding assistant may accelerate development while also creating security risks if outputs are accepted without review.

This is why leadership judgment remains central.

The value of generative AI does not come merely from generating outputs quickly. Value emerges when organizations integrate these capabilities into workflows responsibly and strategically.

In one enterprise workshop involving operations leaders, employees were initially excited by the speed at which AI could generate internal reports. Yet after several weeks, teams realized that much of the generated content still required human validation because managers lacked confidence in the accuracy of AI-produced summaries. The productivity improvement was real, but smaller than initially expected because governance and review processes had not been considered early enough.

Experiences like these explain why many organizations are now shifting their focus from experimentation to operational integration.

The first phase of generative AI adoption was driven largely by curiosity. Organizations wanted to understand what the technology could do. The second phase is much more practical. Leaders now want to understand

- Where measurable business value exists
- Which use cases scale effectively
- How costs can be controlled
- How risks can be managed responsibly

This transition from curiosity to operational value is one of the most important themes in modern enterprise AI adoption.

From a business perspective, generative AI typically creates value in three major ways.

The first is productivity enhancement. Employees complete repetitive cognitive tasks faster, reducing time spent on drafting, summarizing, searching, formatting, or analyzing information.

The second is knowledge accessibility. Generative AI allows organizations to surface information conversationally, reducing dependency on manual searching and fragmented documentation systems.

The third is workflow augmentation. AI systems increasingly assist employees during tasks rather than operating separately from them. Instead of replacing workflows entirely, generative AI becomes embedded within existing tools and daily activities.

A common mistake in enterprise AI programs is assuming automation alone creates transformation. Leaders sometimes assume that generative AI will immediately replace entire functions or departments. In practice, the most successful enterprise implementations are usually those that enhance human capability rather than attempt to eliminate it entirely.

This becomes especially relevant in knowledge-driven industries where judgment, context, compliance, and human interaction remain critical.

Another important leadership consideration is that generative AI is not a single product or capability. It represents a broad category of technologies, platforms, models, and enterprise services. Some solutions are designed for general productivity enhancement, while others support highly customized workflows, industry-specific operations, or enterprise-scale integrations.

This is why organizations must avoid adopting generative AI purely because competitors are doing so. The real leadership challenge is not adopting AI quickly. The challenge is identifying where AI creates sustainable operational value without introducing unnecessary complexity or governance risk.

Figure 2-1 illustrates how generative AI creates value by augmenting human capabilities across everyday enterprise workflows rather than operating as an isolated technology layer.

Figure 2-1. *Generative AI as a Human Capability Multiplier in Enterprise Workflows*

Generative AI vs. Traditional AI

To understand why generative AI is reshaping enterprise strategy so rapidly, it is important to distinguish it from earlier forms of artificial intelligence. Many organizations had already been using AI for years before generative AI entered mainstream business discussions. Recommendation systems, fraud detection models, predictive analytics platforms, intelligent automation tools, and forecasting engines were all part of enterprise AI adoption long before conversational AI assistants became widely accessible.

Yet despite these earlier advancements, generative AI created a level of executive attention and organizational urgency that traditional AI rarely achieved.

The reason lies not only in what the technology can do but in how people interact with it.

Traditional AI systems are typically designed to analyze, classify, predict, or optimize. They operate within relatively defined boundaries and are often trained to perform a narrow task extremely well. For example, a fraud detection system analyzes transaction patterns to identify suspicious behavior. A forecasting model predicts demand trends using historical data. A recommendation engine suggests products based on customer activity.

These systems are highly valuable, but most employees never directly interact with them. The AI operates quietly in the background, influencing decisions or automating processes without becoming part of the everyday user experience.

Generative AI changes this interaction model completely.

Instead of simply analyzing information, generative AI produces new outputs dynamically in response to prompts, instructions, or conversational context. Employees interact with the system directly using natural language, often without requiring technical expertise or specialized training.

This accessibility is one of the defining reasons generative AI spread so quickly across enterprises.

For business leaders, the difference is significant. Traditional AI often required organizations to redesign systems around AI capabilities. Generative AI can frequently integrate into existing workflows more naturally because employees communicate with it conversationally.

This creates a much lower barrier to experimentation.

An employee who may never have used predictive analytics software can still use an AI assistant to summarize meetings, generate drafts, or analyze documents within minutes. As a result, generative AI adoption often begins organically at the workforce level before formal enterprise strategies fully mature.

However, this accessibility also introduces new governance and operational challenges.

Traditional AI systems generally operate within structured outputs and predefined objectives. Their behavior is narrower and often easier to validate operationally. Generative AI systems are probabilistic by nature, meaning responses may vary depending on phrasing, context, or prompt structure. The same request may produce slightly different outputs at different times.

This variability creates concerns that many organizations initially underestimate.

For example, a predictive model used for demand forecasting typically produces measurable outputs within controlled parameters. A generative AI assistant drafting customer communications may generate responses that sound highly convincing while still containing inaccuracies, compliance issues, or inconsistent messaging.

This distinction changes the role of governance significantly.

In traditional AI environments, governance often focused heavily on model accuracy, fairness, and operational reliability. With generative AI, governance must additionally address

- Hallucinations
- Content authenticity
- Responsible usage
- Data exposure risks
- Prompt misuse
- Human oversight

The leadership challenge therefore becomes broader than technology selection alone.

Another important difference lies in the nature of business value created by these systems.

Traditional AI usually creates value through optimization and prediction. It improves operational efficiency by helping organizations make better decisions based on structured historical data. Generative AI, however, often creates value through augmentation. It assists employees directly during knowledge work, reducing repetitive cognitive effort and accelerating content-related activities.

This distinction may appear subtle initially, but operationally it changes where organizations experience impact first.

Traditional AI initiatives often began within technical or analytical departments because specialized expertise was required to build and maintain models. Generative AI initiatives frequently begin inside business functions themselves because users can experiment with AI capabilities directly.

In one enterprise transformation program, the first successful AI deployment was not a large predictive analytics platform but a simple generative AI assistant that reduced time spent creating internal compliance summaries. Technically, the solution was far less sophisticated than earlier AI initiatives the organization had explored. Operationally, however, it delivered faster adoption and clearer workforce impact because employees interacted with it naturally within their daily routines.

This illustrates an important leadership lesson.

The most technically advanced AI solution is not always the one that creates the greatest organizational value.

Generative AI also differs from traditional AI in the speed at which value expectations emerge. Predictive AI initiatives often required extended implementation cycles, significant data preparation, and specialized deployment efforts before business impact became visible. Generative AI systems can sometimes demonstrate visible results within hours or days.

While this accelerates enthusiasm, it can also create unrealistic expectations.

Leaders may assume that because initial demonstrations appear impressive, enterprise-scale transformation will happen equally quickly. In practice, scaling generative AI responsibly across large organizations introduces challenges related to governance, adoption, integration, security, cost management, and operational oversight.

This explains why many organizations are currently transitioning from experimental AI usage toward platform-based AI strategies. Increasingly, enterprise AI adoption is moving beyond isolated tools and toward integrated ecosystems involving copilots, enterprise knowledge systems, AI orchestration platforms, and grounded AI experiences connected to organizational data.

Microsoft's evolving AI ecosystem reflects this shift through platforms such as Microsoft 365 Copilot, Copilot Studio, Azure AI services, and Azure AI Foundry, where AI capabilities are increasingly positioned as embedded enterprise productivity and workflow capabilities rather than stand-alone technologies.

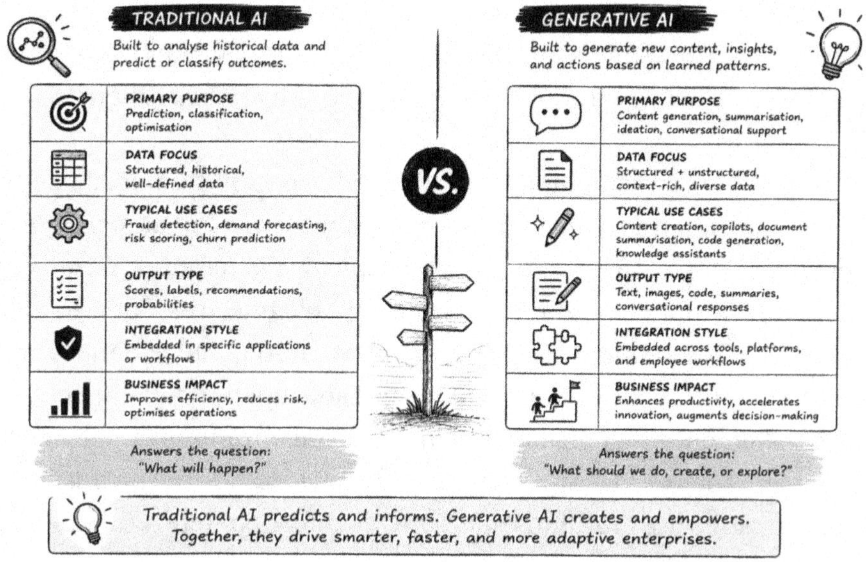

***Figure 2-2.** Traditional AI vs. Generative AI in Enterprise Environments*

Figure 2-2 illustrates how traditional AI primarily focuses on prediction, classification, and optimization, whereas generative AI focuses on augmentation, content creation, and conversational interaction across enterprise workflows.

Typical Enterprise Use Cases and Value Drivers

One of the reasons generative AI gained rapid enterprise attention is that organizations could immediately identify practical use cases across multiple business functions. Unlike earlier AI initiatives that often required specialized data science teams and lengthy implementation cycles, generative AI demonstrated visible value within existing workflows almost immediately.

Employees did not need to understand machine learning models to experience productivity improvements. They simply interacted with AI systems using natural language and began applying them to everyday tasks.

This ease of experimentation accelerated adoption significantly.

However, an important leadership challenge emerged alongside this enthusiasm. Many organizations began deploying generative AI broadly without clearly understanding where sustainable business value actually existed. Initial excitement often focused on what AI could generate rather than whether those outputs created measurable operational impact.

That difference matters more than many organizations initially realize.

The presence of AI activity does not automatically indicate business transformation. Organizations may generate more content, automate more interactions, or increase workflow speed without necessarily improving strategic outcomes.

Strong AI Transformation Leaders therefore focus less on novelty and more on value drivers.

The question is not:

"Where can we use AI?"

The more important question is:

"Where does AI reduce friction, improve decisions, accelerate workflows, or create measurable organizational advantage?"

This shift in thinking changes how enterprise AI opportunities should be evaluated.

Understanding Enterprise Value Drivers

Although generative AI use cases vary widely across industries, most successful implementations tend to create value through a relatively small number of recurring patterns.

The first and most immediate value driver is productivity enhancement.

Many enterprise workflows contain repetitive cognitive activities that consume significant employee time without directly creating strategic value. Employees repeatedly summarize information, draft documents, search for knowledge, prepare communications, review reports, and consolidate updates across systems.

Generative AI reduces friction within these activities.

For example:

- Customer service teams can generate response drafts faster.
- Legal teams can summarize contracts.
- HR departments can accelerate policy communication.
- Consultants can prepare proposal outlines.
- Developers can generate code suggestions or documentation.

These improvements may appear incremental individually, but at organizational scale, they become highly significant.

In many enterprises, the first measurable AI gains are not transformational innovations. They are reductions in repetitive knowledge work.

This is one reason productivity-focused AI deployments often succeed earlier than highly ambitious transformation programs.

The second major value driver is knowledge accessibility.

Large organizations frequently struggle with fragmented information. Employees spend substantial time searching for documents, locating expertise, navigating disconnected systems, or interpreting complex internal processes. Generative AI systems connected to enterprise knowledge sources can reduce this friction dramatically by allowing employees to retrieve and interact with information conversationally.

This changes how knowledge flows within organizations.

Instead of relying solely on static documentation systems, employees can increasingly interact with organizational knowledge dynamically through AI-assisted experiences. This is especially valuable in environments where information changes rapidly or where employees need quick contextual guidance.

The third value driver is workflow acceleration.

Generative AI increasingly operates as an embedded assistant within daily workflows rather than as a separate application. Employees no longer stop their work to access specialized systems. Instead, AI capabilities appear directly inside collaboration platforms, productivity tools, development environments, and enterprise applications.

This integration model is strategically important because adoption becomes easier when AI aligns naturally with existing employee behavior.

In practice, organizations often underestimate how important workflow integration is for long-term adoption success.

Technically impressive AI systems frequently fail because employees perceive them as additional tools requiring extra effort. Simpler AI capabilities embedded directly into familiar workflows often achieve stronger adoption even when their functionality is less advanced.

Common Enterprise Use Cases

Although generative AI use cases continue evolving rapidly, several categories consistently appear across industries.

Content Generation and Communication

This remains one of the most widely adopted enterprise use cases.

Employees spend considerable time drafting emails, preparing reports, creating presentations, summarizing meetings, writing proposals, or generating internal documentation. Generative AI accelerates these activities significantly.

The value here is usually not complete automation. Most enterprise environments still require human review, contextual judgment, and approval processes. Instead, the value comes from reducing initial drafting effort and accelerating information preparation.

In one consulting engagement, teams discovered that AI-generated first drafts reduced proposal preparation time substantially, even though final review and editing remained fully human led. The operational benefit emerged not from eliminating expertise but from reducing repetitive preparation effort.

This distinction is important because organizations sometimes overestimate the maturity of fully autonomous content generation.

In reality, many successful deployments operate as augmentation systems rather than replacement systems.

Enterprise Knowledge Assistants

Another rapidly expanding use case involves conversational access to organizational knowledge.

Employees often struggle to locate policies, technical guidance, operational procedures, or historical project information spread across multiple systems. Generative AI assistants grounded on enterprise data can help employees retrieve relevant information conversationally instead of manually searching through fragmented repositories.

This can improve

- Onboarding speed
- Employee productivity
- Support efficiency
- Operational consistency

However, this use case also introduces governance complexity because enterprise knowledge systems may contain sensitive, confidential, or outdated information. Leaders must therefore balance accessibility with security and compliance requirements carefully.

Software Development Assistance

Generative AI is also reshaping software development workflows significantly.

AI coding assistants can

- Generate code suggestions
- Explain functions
- Identify errors
- Accelerate testing
- Support documentation creation

The productivity impact here can be substantial, particularly for repetitive development activities.

Yet leadership teams should avoid assuming that AI-generated code automatically improves software quality. In practice, development teams still require strong review, security validation, architectural oversight, and testing disciplines.

The most effective implementations usually combine AI acceleration with strong engineering governance rather than replacing engineering discipline altogether.

Customer Service and Support

Customer service functions are increasingly using generative AI for

- Response drafting
- Conversational assistance
- Summarization
- Intelligent routing
- Agent support

In many cases, AI operates alongside human agents rather than replacing them entirely.

This hybrid model is often operationally effective because customer interactions frequently require empathy, contextual understanding, escalation judgment, and regulatory awareness that fully autonomous systems still struggle to manage consistently.

For leaders, the important lesson is that AI value often emerges through augmentation of human capability rather than complete process replacement.

The Risk of Chasing Generic Use Cases

As generative AI adoption accelerates, organizations increasingly face pressure to replicate use cases announced by competitors or industry peers. This creates a common mistake: pursuing AI initiatives because they appear innovative rather than because they solve meaningful organizational problems.

In some situations, organizations achieve better outcomes through process simplification, stronger governance, or conventional automation rather than introducing generative AI unnecessarily.

Strong transformation leaders therefore avoid evaluating AI opportunities in isolation. Instead, they assess whether AI is genuinely the most appropriate solution for the problem being addressed.

This mindset is heavily reflected in AB-731-style decision scenarios.

The exam consistently rewards practical, context-aware decisions over technically ambitious but operationally unnecessary solutions.

Evaluating Use Cases Through a Leadership Lens

One useful way to evaluate enterprise AI opportunities is to assess them across three dimensions simultaneously:

- Operational friction
- Scalability
- Organizational readiness

High-value opportunities usually involve repetitive cognitive effort, clear productivity bottlenecks, accessible workflows, and environments where employees are already comfortable using digital tools.

By contrast, AI initiatives often struggle when

- Objectives are unclear
- Governance is weak
- Workflows are poorly understood
- Organizational trust is low

This explains why some apparently simple AI use cases scale successfully while technically sophisticated initiatives fail to move beyond pilot stages.

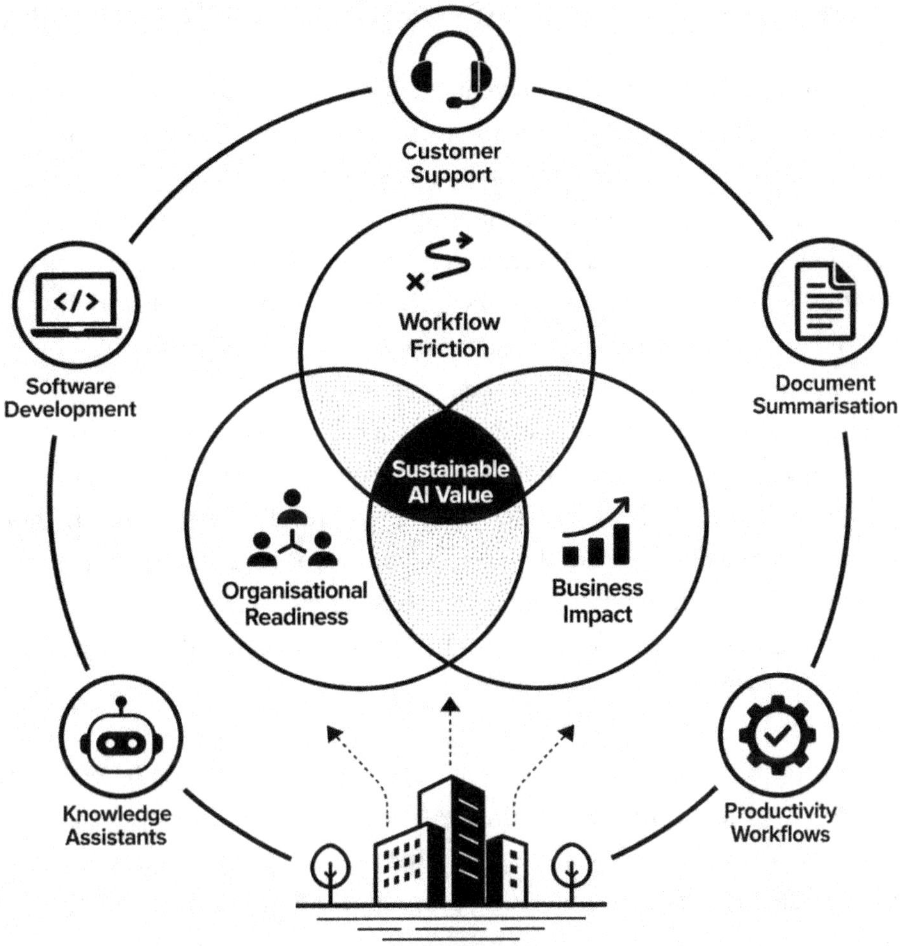

***Figure 2-3.** Enterprise AI Value Drivers and Use Case Alignment*

Figure 2-3 illustrates how sustainable AI value emerges when enterprise use cases align with operational friction points, workforce readiness, and measurable business outcomes.

Productivity Gains vs. Innovation Outcomes

One of the reasons generative AI created such immediate excitement across industries is that organizations were able to observe visible productivity improvements almost instantly. Employees who previously spent hours preparing reports, summarizing meetings, drafting emails, reviewing documents, or searching for information suddenly found that many of these activities could be accelerated significantly through AI-assisted workflows.

For leadership teams, this created a powerful first impression.

Unlike earlier enterprise technologies that often required long implementation cycles before delivering measurable value, generative AI produced visible outputs immediately. Teams could experience the impact directly within their daily work. Meetings were summarized faster, presentations were drafted more quickly, developers received coding assistance in real time, and employees reduced time spent on repetitive knowledge tasks.

This explains why productivity enhancement became the first major business case for generative AI adoption.

In many organizations, the earliest AI successes were not ambitious transformation programs or large-scale strategic reinventions. They were relatively simple improvements that reduced friction within everyday work. Employees spent less time preparing repetitive content and more time focusing on activities requiring judgment, collaboration, customer interaction, or decision-making.

At enterprise scale, even these seemingly modest improvements can become highly significant.

A few minutes saved across recurring workflows may appear minor when viewed individually. Yet when multiplied across thousands of employees and operational processes, the cumulative impact becomes substantial. This is one reason productivity-focused AI initiatives are often commercially attractive. They generate measurable operational value quickly and help organizations build confidence in AI adoption without requiring immediate large-scale organizational change.

However, one of the most important leadership mistakes is assuming that productivity improvement automatically represents transformation.

An organization may complete tasks faster while still operating fundamentally the same way it did before AI adoption. Reports may be generated more efficiently, meetings may be summarized more quickly, and communication workflows may become smoother, but the organization's underlying operating model, decision structure, and strategic capability may remain largely unchanged.

Many organizations mistakenly treat productivity gains as evidence of transformation.

Productivity gains improve how efficiently work is performed. Innovation outcomes change how the organization itself creates value.

In practice, many enterprises initially remain focused on task acceleration because it is easier to implement and easier to measure. Existing workflows continue operating largely as before, with AI acting as an assistant layered onto current processes. Employees become more efficient, but the broader structure of the organization remains stable.

Transformation begins when organizations rethink the workflow itself rather than simply accelerating individual tasks within it.

For example, using AI to generate customer support summaries improves operational efficiency. Redesigning the entire customer engagement process around AI-assisted resolution, knowledge retrieval, and proactive support changes the operating model itself. Similarly, accelerating document preparation improves productivity, but enabling AI-assisted operational decision-making across departments begins reshaping how the organization functions strategically.

The difference is not merely technical. It reflects a deeper organizational shift.

In many enterprise environments, leaders initially overestimate how quickly transformational outcomes will emerge because the early demonstrations feel so impressive. Generative AI creates the appearance of rapid transformation because outputs are immediate and highly visible. Yet real organizational transformation usually occurs much more gradually.

Technology adoption alone rarely changes how organizations operate.

Transformation requires operational redesign, governance maturity, leadership alignment, workforce adaptation, and cultural readiness. Without these elements, organizations often remain trapped in isolated productivity experiments that generate local improvements without producing broader strategic impact.

In one enterprise transformation discussion, leadership teams were highly encouraged by the efficiency gains employees achieved using AI-generated reporting and internal documentation tools. Employees completed repetitive tasks faster, and operational workloads reduced noticeably. However, several months later, the organization realized that approval bottlenecks, fragmented workflows, and decision delays remained largely unchanged. Productivity had improved, but organizational agility had not evolved to the same extent.

This pattern is common across many early-stage AI programs.

The first wave of value usually emerges through efficiency. The second wave emerges only when organizations begin redesigning workflows and decision models around AI-assisted capabilities.

That second stage is significantly more difficult because it introduces broader organizational questions. Leaders must determine how responsibilities change, how governance evolves, how trust is maintained, and how AI-assisted decisions integrate into existing operational structures.

This is why many organizations approach AI adoption progressively. Early initiatives focus on productivity improvement because they create measurable value quickly and help employees become comfortable with AI-assisted work. Over time, as operational maturity improves, organizations begin exploring broader innovation opportunities that reshape customer experiences, collaboration models, or strategic decision-making processes.

The sequence matters more than many leaders initially realize.

Attempting large-scale transformation before the organization is operationally prepared often creates resistance, unrealistic expectations, and governance challenges. By contrast, organizations that build maturity gradually tend to develop stronger adoption patterns and more sustainable long-term outcomes.

Another important leadership reality is that visible AI activity should not automatically be interpreted as innovation. Some organizations deploy multiple AI tools, launch numerous pilots, and generate large volumes of AI-assisted content without materially improving competitive advantage or operational effectiveness.

This creates the illusion of transformation without delivering meaningful strategic change.

Strong AI Transformation Leaders therefore distinguish carefully between experimentation, productivity improvement, and genuine organizational innovation. All three are valuable, but they represent different stages of AI maturity and should not be confused with one another.

This distinction is reflected heavily in Exam AB-731. The exam consistently favors balanced leadership decisions that align AI adoption with realistic business value, operational readiness, and sustainable organizational outcomes rather than purely ambitious technological thinking.

Ultimately, the most successful enterprise AI strategies are rarely those focused exclusively on either productivity or transformation. Sustainable value usually emerges when organizations balance both horizons simultaneously. Short-term productivity improvements create operational momentum and measurable returns, while longer-term innovation initiatives gradually reshape how the organization operates and competes.

Figure 2-4 illustrates how organizations typically progress from AI experimentation and productivity enhancement toward workflow integration, innovation, and broader business transformation as organizational AI maturity evolves.

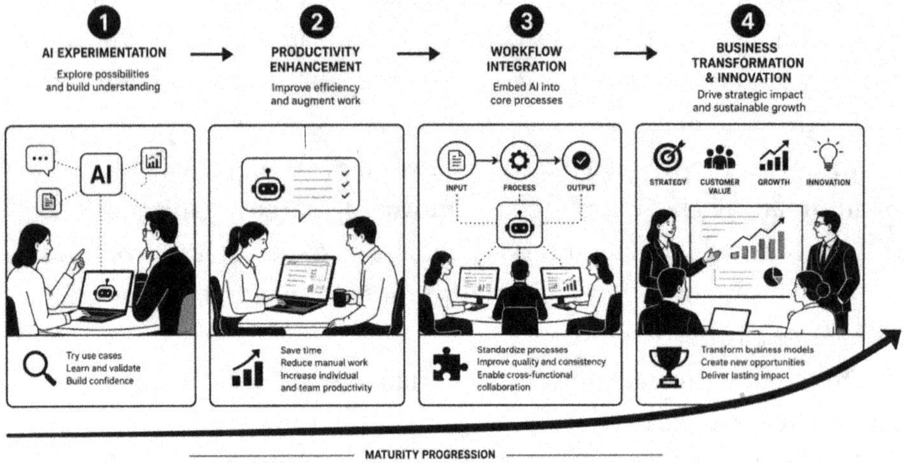

Figure 2-4. *From Productivity Gains to AI-Driven Transformation*

Cost Considerations and ROI Thinking

As organizations move beyond experimentation and begin integrating generative AI into daily operations, the conversation gradually changes. Early discussions are usually driven by curiosity and excitement. Teams explore what AI can generate, how quickly tasks can be completed, and where immediate productivity improvements appear possible. Over time, however, leadership attention shifts toward a far more practical question: does the long-term business value justify the cost, complexity, and operational change required to sustain AI adoption at scale?

This is where many organizations begin to realize that enterprise AI transformation is not simply a technology initiative. It is an operational investment that affects workflows, governance models, employee behavior, and decision-making processes across the organization.

In the early stages of adoption, generative AI often appears highly cost-effective because the visible results emerge quickly. Employees can draft documents faster, summarize information within seconds, or automate repetitive knowledge tasks with relatively little effort. These early gains create momentum and help organizations recognize the practical potential of AI-assisted work.

However, scaling those capabilities across enterprise environments introduces a very different set of realities.

What initially appears to be a simple AI deployment gradually expands into broader organizational considerations. Security teams begin evaluating data exposure risks. Compliance functions become concerned about governance and content validation. Technology teams assess integration requirements across existing systems. Business leaders start questioning whether employees are genuinely saving time or simply shifting effort into reviewing and validating AI-generated outputs.

This is usually the stage where enterprise excitement meets operational reality.

In one enterprise advisory discussion, leadership teams were initially impressed by how quickly AI-generated summaries reduced documentation effort during pilot phases. Yet several months later, managers realized that employees still needed significant review time because the organization lacked confidence in the consistency and reliability of AI-generated outputs. Productivity had improved, but not to the extent originally projected. The challenge was not the technology itself. The challenge was operational trust.

This is one of the most important realities of enterprise generative AI adoption. Theoretical productivity gains do not always translate directly into sustainable business value.

Strong AI Transformation Leaders therefore avoid evaluating AI investments purely through excitement, technical capability, or demonstration quality. Instead, they focus on whether the technology creates measurable and repeatable operational improvement over time.

That evaluation requires a broader understanding of return on investment.

Many organizations initially approach AI ROI from a traditional cost-reduction mindset. They attempt to calculate how many hours can be saved, how much manual effort can be reduced, or how operational efficiency can improve. While these measurements are important, they rarely capture the full value of generative AI.

In practice, generative AI often creates value indirectly.

An employee who spends less time preparing reports may spend more time engaging with customers or improving decision quality. Faster access to organizational knowledge may accelerate collaboration between teams. AI-assisted workflows may reduce delays that previously slowed operational execution. Some benefits become measurable financially, while others influence organizational agility, responsiveness, and workforce effectiveness in ways that are harder to quantify immediately.

This makes generative AI fundamentally different from many traditional technology investments.

The value often emerges cumulatively through hundreds of small operational improvements rather than one dramatic transformational event. A few minutes saved across recurring tasks may appear insignificant in isolation, but when multiplied across large enterprise environments, the cumulative impact becomes substantial.

At the same time, leaders must remain disciplined enough to avoid exaggerating those benefits.

One of the common patterns in enterprise AI adoption is the tendency to overestimate efficiency gains during the early stages of deployment. Demonstrations frequently create the impression that AI can fully automate knowledge work, when in reality many enterprise workflows still require human judgment, validation, and contextual understanding.

This is particularly important in regulated industries or environments involving sensitive information, where employees may still need to verify AI-generated content carefully before using it operationally.

As organizations mature in their AI adoption journey, they also begin recognizing that cost structures become more complex over time. Early pilots are usually controlled and limited in scale. Once AI becomes embedded within daily workflows across departments and business functions, usage patterns expand rapidly. Consumption increases, integrations become deeper, and governance requirements grow alongside adoption.

The technology itself may represent only one part of the investment equation.

Operational readiness, employee enablement, workflow redesign, security oversight, and governance maturity gradually become equally important contributors to long-term sustainability. In some organizations, the effort required to integrate AI responsibly into existing business processes becomes more challenging than the deployment of the AI capability itself.

This explains why some technically successful AI pilots struggle to scale operationally.

The issue is rarely whether the AI works. More often, the challenge is whether the organization is prepared to absorb the operational change surrounding it.

Leaders therefore need to think carefully about the relationship between business value and operational complexity. Not every use case requires highly sophisticated AI architecture. In many situations, simpler AI-assisted workflows integrated naturally into existing tools may create stronger ROI than highly customized platforms that introduce significant maintenance and governance overhead.

Interestingly, some of the most effective enterprise AI programs are not the most technically ambitious ones.

Rather than attempting large-scale transformation immediately, organizations usually progress through stages of maturity. Early initiatives focus on productivity enhancement and operational efficiency. Over time, as governance models strengthen and workforce confidence improves, organizations begin exploring broader workflow redesign and strategic innovation opportunities.

This gradual progression is far more sustainable than attempting organization-wide transformation too early.

Another important leadership consideration is that AI ROI should evolve alongside organizational maturity. During early adoption phases, success may be measured through employee usage patterns, operational efficiency improvements, or reductions in repetitive effort. Later, organizations begin evaluating broader outcomes such as customer experience improvement, decision quality, operational agility, and competitive differentiation.

These outcomes emerge at different stages and should not be evaluated using identical expectations.

One of the most common mistakes leaders make is expecting transformational business outcomes immediately after deploying productivity-oriented AI tools. In reality, transformation usually follows operational maturity rather than preceding it.

This is why strong AI Transformation Leaders remain patient, disciplined, and realistic about AI adoption timelines.

They understand that sustainable enterprise value rarely comes from technology capability alone. It emerges when organizational readiness, governance maturity, workforce adoption, and operational integration evolve together in a balanced manner.

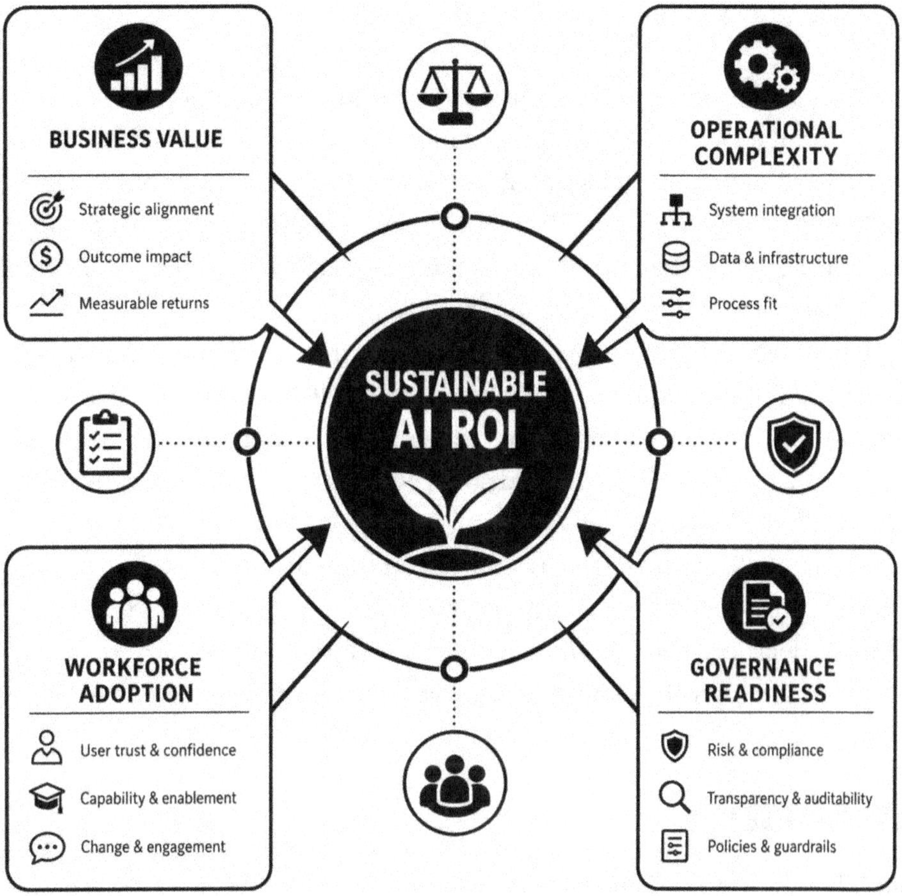

***Figure 2-5.** Balancing Cost, Complexity, and Sustainable AI Value*

Figure 2-5 illustrates how sustainable AI ROI emerges when business value, operational complexity, workforce adoption, and governance readiness remain balanced rather than being treated as isolated considerations.

Leader's Lens

Many organizations initially approach generative AI as a technology deployment exercise. In practice, the most successful AI initiatives rarely begin with ambitious transformation goals or highly sophisticated implementations. They usually begin by removing friction from existing workflows in ways that employees can immediately experience and trust.

This is an important leadership mindset.

Employees adopt AI more naturally when the technology simplifies work rather than disrupts it unnecessarily. A well-integrated AI assistant that reduces repetitive effort often creates more sustainable organizational value than a technically advanced solution that introduces operational complexity without clear business impact.

Strong AI Transformation Leaders therefore focus less on deploying the most advanced AI capability and more on identifying where AI can improve decision-making, reduce operational friction, and support employees responsibly within real business environments.

Summary

This chapter explored generative AI from the perspective of business value, organizational impact, and leadership decision-making rather than purely technical capability. The discussion began by examining why generative AI gained rapid enterprise attention and how its accessibility changed the way organizations interact with AI technologies. Unlike earlier AI systems that often operated invisibly within specialized analytical environments, generative AI became directly accessible to employees across departments through natural language interactions and AI-assisted workflows.

The chapter also examined the distinction between generative AI and traditional AI systems. Traditional AI primarily focuses on prediction, classification, optimization, and analytical processing, whereas generative

AI introduces conversational interaction, content generation, and workflow augmentation. This difference is important because it changes not only how organizations use AI but also how employees experience and adopt it operationally.

Another key theme throughout the chapter was the importance of evaluating AI initiatives through a business lens rather than through technology enthusiasm alone. Enterprise AI adoption succeeds when organizations identify practical use cases aligned with operational friction points, workforce readiness, and measurable business outcomes. Generative AI creates value most effectively when it reduces repetitive cognitive effort, improves knowledge accessibility, accelerates workflows, and supports employees within existing operational environments.

At the same time, the chapter highlighted that productivity improvement and transformation are not identical outcomes. Many organizations initially experience value through operational efficiency and task acceleration. True transformation occurs later, when organizations redesign workflows, decision models, and business processes around AI-assisted capabilities. This distinction is critical because early productivity gains often create the operational maturity required for broader innovation later.

The discussion on cost considerations and ROI further reinforced the importance of balanced leadership thinking. Sustainable AI value does not emerge purely from technical capability or rapid experimentation. It depends on whether organizations can balance business impact with governance readiness, workforce adoption, operational complexity, and long-term scalability. Leaders must therefore evaluate AI initiatives realistically, recognizing that successful enterprise AI adoption is as much an organizational challenge as it is a technological one.

For many organizations, generative AI still feels like a moving target. New tools, platforms, and capabilities continue appearing rapidly, which often creates pressure to adopt AI quickly. Yet in real enterprise environments, successful adoption is rarely driven by urgency alone.

The organizations creating meaningful value are usually the ones applying AI carefully, learning progressively, and aligning adoption with operational realities rather than market hype.

Taken together, this chapter emphasizes a central idea that appears repeatedly throughout Exam AB-731: successful AI transformation is rarely about deploying the most advanced technology first. It is about applying AI thoughtfully, responsibly, and in ways that align with real organizational priorities and operational realities.

As the next chapter shifts toward risks, ethics, and responsible AI leadership, this balanced decision-making mindset becomes even more important. The rapid adoption of generative AI creates significant opportunities, but it also introduces challenges related to trust, governance, security, bias, compliance, and organizational accountability. Understanding what AI can achieve is valuable, but understanding how to apply it responsibly and sustainably is what ultimately defines an effective AI Transformation Leader. Figure 2-6 summarizes how organizations typically progress from early AI experimentation toward sustainable business value and transformation.

***Figure 2-6.** From AI Experimentation to Sustainable Business Value*

Exam-Style Questions

Question 1

A retail company's leadership team wants to roll out generative AI quickly after noticing competitors publicly announcing AI initiatives. However, the organization still lacks clear governance policies, employee readiness programs, and well-defined business use cases.

What should leadership focus on first?

A. Expanding AI deployment immediately across all departments

B. Building custom AI models before defining business goals

C. Establishing governance, workforce readiness, and clear business objectives

D. Avoiding AI adoption until every operational risk is eliminated

Correct Answer

C

Explanation

The scenario highlights a common enterprise challenge: enthusiasm moving faster than organizational readiness. In AB-731-style questions, the strongest answer is usually the one that balances innovation with governance, adoption planning, and measurable business outcomes.

Question 2

A financial services organization introduces generative AI to help teams summarize internal reports. Employees save time, but managers still insist on manually reviewing all AI-generated summaries before using them operationally.

Which statement best describes the organization's current stage of AI adoption?

A. The organization has completed AI transformation

B. The organization is seeing productivity improvement rather than full transformation

C. The AI initiative has failed because human review is still required

D. Employees should stop validating AI-generated content to improve efficiency

Correct Answer

B

Explanation

The organization is improving operational efficiency, but workflows and decision structures still depend heavily on human oversight. This reflects augmentation and productivity enhancement rather than deeper organizational transformation.

Question 3

A leadership team is evaluating two AI initiatives. One proposal involves a highly customized AI platform requiring significant integration effort and operational oversight. The second is a simpler AI assistant integrated into existing productivity tools with lower complexity.

Which option is more likely to create measurable business value more quickly?

A. The highly customized platform because it appears more innovative

B. The integrated AI assistant because adoption and operational alignment are easier

C. Both solutions will produce identical organizational outcomes

D. Neither initiative should move forward until proprietary AI models are developed internally

Correct Answer

B

Explanation

AB-731 often rewards practical decision-making over technical ambition. Simpler solutions aligned with existing workflows frequently create faster adoption and clearer ROI than highly complex implementations.

Question 4

An organization uses generative AI to accelerate internal documentation and reporting activities. Employees complete tasks faster, but customer experiences, business workflows, and operational structures remain largely unchanged.

What does this scenario primarily represent?

A. Enterprise-wide transformation

B. Productivity improvement

C. Governance failure

D. Predictive analytics optimization

Correct Answer

B

Explanation

The organization is improving efficiency within existing workflows, but broader business operations have not fundamentally changed. This reflects productivity gains rather than transformational innovation.

Question 5

A company plans to introduce enterprise knowledge assistants connected to internal organizational data. Leadership is concerned about employees receiving inaccurate information or exposing sensitive business content unintentionally.

What should leadership prioritize?

A. Expanding AI access rapidly to maximize adoption

B. Removing human oversight to improve efficiency

C. Governance controls, data security, and grounded AI responses

D. Replacing all existing knowledge systems immediately

Correct Answer

C

Explanation

As enterprise AI systems become connected to organizational data, governance, trust, and responsible information handling become critical leadership concerns.

Question 6

A manufacturing company introduces AI-assisted maintenance documentation for engineering teams. Employees appreciate the time savings, but some managers worry that engineers may rely too heavily on AI-generated recommendations without validating them properly.

What is the most appropriate leadership response?

A. Remove AI access from engineering teams entirely

B. Encourage unrestricted AI usage to maximize productivity gains

C. Introduce responsible AI guidance and human validation processes

D. Replace all existing engineering review processes with AI automation

Correct Answer

C

Explanation

The goal is not to eliminate AI usage but to ensure it is applied responsibly. Human oversight remains important in environments where operational accuracy and safety are critical.

Question 7

An organization successfully deploys AI assistants inside collaboration platforms, and employee adoption increases rapidly. However, executives struggle to determine whether the organization is creating measurable long-term value.

What should leadership focus on next?

A. Expanding AI usage externally before evaluating outcomes

B. Defining measurable operational and business success metrics

C. Replacing existing governance processes with AI automation

D. Building proprietary large language models immediately

Correct Answer

B

Explanation

High adoption alone does not confirm business value. Leaders need clear metrics tied to operational improvement, efficiency, customer impact, or strategic outcomes.

Question 8

A healthcare provider is evaluating a generative AI solution designed to support patient interactions. The platform appears highly capable, but leadership cannot clearly determine how patient information is processed or governed.

What should leadership prioritize during evaluation?

A. Selecting the most advanced AI capability available

B. Accelerating deployment timelines before competitors adopt similar tools

C. Ensuring governance, transparency, and compliance requirements are addressed

D. Avoiding AI adoption entirely within healthcare environments

Correct Answer

C

Explanation

In regulated industries, leadership decisions must balance innovation with trust, transparency, compliance, and responsible data management practices.

Question 9

A company launches multiple AI pilots across departments, but very few initiatives move beyond experimentation into operational deployment. Employees remain interested in AI, yet measurable business outcomes remain limited.

What is the most likely issue?

A. Employees are adopting AI too quickly

B. The organization lacks operational alignment and adoption strategy

C. Generative AI is unsuitable for enterprise environments

D. AI should only be used within technical departments

Correct Answer

B

Explanation

Many organizations experience strong experimentation activity but struggle to operationalize AI because governance, business alignment, adoption planning, and workflow integration are not fully established.

Question 10

A leadership team wants to encourage AI-driven innovation but is concerned that introducing too many governance controls may slow experimentation and reduce employee enthusiasm.

What is the most balanced approach?

A. Remove governance controls to accelerate innovation

B. Delay all AI adoption until governance frameworks become fully mature

C. Encourage innovation while introducing phased governance and responsible AI practices

D. Restrict AI usage permanently to specialized technical teams only

Correct Answer

C

Explanation

Strong AI leadership requires balancing innovation with responsibility. Sustainable enterprise adoption depends on encouraging experimentation while maintaining governance, accountability, and operational trust.

CHAPTER 3

Risks, Ethics, and Responsible AI Leadership

Introduction

As generative AI adoption accelerates across industries, organizations are beginning to realize that the real challenge is no longer access to AI capability. The technology is already widely available. Employees can generate content, automate repetitive tasks, summarize information, and interact with AI systems more easily than ever before.

The harder question is whether organizations can use these capabilities responsibly.

In the early stages of AI adoption, many enterprise discussions focus heavily on opportunity, productivity, and innovation. Over time, however, a different set of concerns starts emerging. Leadership teams begin asking what happens when AI-generated information is inaccurate, biased, misleading, noncompliant, or used in ways that were never originally intended.

These concerns are not theoretical.

K. Shaikh, *Microsoft Certified: AI Transformation Leader Study Companion*, Certification Study Companion Series, https://doi.org/10.1007/979-8-8688-3168-3_3

Many organizations initially treat issues such as hallucinations, bias, or misuse as isolated technical limitations. That perception usually changes once AI-generated outputs begin influencing customer interactions, operational decisions, regulatory processes, or public-facing communication. At that point, AI risk becomes a leadership issue rather than simply a technical one.

This shift is important because generative AI behaves differently from traditional enterprise systems. Conventional business applications are usually designed around predictable workflows and predefined outputs. Generative AI systems operate probabilistically. They generate responses dynamically based on patterns, context, and prompts, which means outputs may vary, contain inaccuracies, or produce unintended results even when the system appears highly confident.

For organizations, this creates a new kind of operational challenge.

The risk is not only that AI may fail technically. The greater concern is that employees or customers may trust AI-generated outputs too quickly without fully understanding their limitations. In many enterprise environments, the issue is not whether AI can generate content. It is whether the organization has established enough governance, oversight, and accountability to use that content responsibly.

This is where Responsible AI becomes essential.

Responsible AI is not simply about compliance documentation or governance frameworks. At its core, it is about ensuring that AI systems operate in ways that remain trustworthy, transparent, safe, and aligned with organizational values. As AI becomes more deeply integrated into business operations, leaders must balance innovation with accountability, operational speed with governance, and automation with human oversight.

Over time, many organizations discover that trust becomes one of the most difficult aspects of enterprise AI adoption. Employees may initially embrace AI enthusiastically, but confidence can decline rapidly if systems generate inaccurate information, expose sensitive data, or behave inconsistently across workflows. Trust, once lost in enterprise AI systems, is difficult to rebuild quickly.

This chapter explores how leaders should think about AI risk, ethics, governance, and responsible decision-making in enterprise environments. It examines the limitations of generative AI, the principles behind Microsoft's Responsible AI approach, the growing importance of transparency and accountability, and the increasing role of regulatory and compliance awareness in AI strategy discussions.

Most importantly, the chapter focuses on developing a practical leadership mindset for evaluating AI risk realistically rather than reactively. Responsible AI leadership is not about slowing innovation unnecessarily. It is about ensuring that organizations adopt AI in ways that remain sustainable, trustworthy, and operationally responsible over time.

Limitations of Generative AI (Bias, Hallucinations, and Misuse)

One of the reasons generative AI feels so powerful is that its responses often appear highly fluent, confident, and contextually relevant. In many situations, the output can sound remarkably convincing, even when the underlying information is incomplete, inaccurate, or entirely fabricated.

That creates a dangerous illusion.

Unlike traditional enterprise systems that operate within relatively predictable rules and structured outputs, generative AI systems generate responses probabilistically. They do not "understand" information in the same way humans do. Instead, they predict patterns based on training data, prompts, and context. As a result, the system may produce responses that sound authoritative while still being factually wrong.

Many organizations initially underestimate this behavior.

During early experimentation phases, hallucinations are often treated as minor technical imperfections or amusing AI mistakes. That perception usually changes once AI-generated outputs begin influencing customer interactions, executive reporting, operational decisions, or compliance-related communication. At that point, the consequences become much more serious.

One of the more uncomfortable realities of generative AI is that systems can generate incorrect information with a high degree of confidence. Microsoft and other AI providers openly acknowledge hallucinations as one of the major challenges associated with large language models and generative AI systems.

In enterprise environments, the issue is rarely just technical accuracy. The larger concern is misplaced trust.

Employees often assume that polished AI-generated responses are reliable simply because they appear professional and coherent. Over time, this can create operational dependency on outputs that may not always be validated properly.

In one enterprise workshop, a team used AI-generated summaries to accelerate internal reporting cycles. Initially, the productivity improvements appeared impressive. However, managers later discovered that several reports contained subtle factual inaccuracies that employees had overlooked because the language itself sounded highly credible. The problem was not malicious behavior by the system. The problem was overreliance without sufficient verification.

That pattern is becoming increasingly common across industries.

Hallucinations are not always obvious. Some AI-generated inaccuracies are easy to detect because they appear unrealistic or inconsistent. Others are much harder to identify because they contain partial truths mixed with fabricated details. Those situations are operationally far more dangerous because they reduce the likelihood of human scrutiny.

This is one reason Responsible AI discussions increasingly focus on grounded AI systems, retrieval-based approaches, and human oversight models designed to reduce hallucination risks.

However, hallucinations represent only one part of the broader challenge.

Bias remains another significant concern in generative AI systems. Large language models are trained on enormous volumes of publicly available and organizational data. Those datasets inevitably contain historical biases, cultural imbalances, stereotypes, and uneven representation patterns. AI systems may therefore reproduce or amplify problematic assumptions that already exist within the data itself.

Sometimes these biases appear subtly rather than explicitly.

For example, an AI recruitment assistant may unintentionally favor certain language styles associated with specific demographics. A content generation system may produce stereotypical assumptions about professions, regions, or social groups. Customer-facing AI systems may respond inconsistently depending on phrasing, language patterns, or contextual cues.

These issues are not always deliberate or visible immediately. In many cases, organizations discover bias only after systems are already being used operationally.

This is where Responsible AI becomes much more than a technical conversation. It becomes an organizational accountability issue.

Microsoft's Responsible AI principles specifically emphasize fairness, reliability and safety, privacy and security, inclusiveness, transparency, and accountability as foundational considerations for AI systems.

What makes generative AI particularly challenging is that these risks often emerge dynamically after deployment rather than remaining confined to model development stages alone.

Traditional enterprise applications usually behave consistently once tested and deployed. Generative AI systems continue interacting with unpredictable prompts, evolving business contexts, and changing operational environments. This means organizations cannot treat Responsible AI as a one-time compliance exercise completed during implementation.

Governance becomes continuous.

Another area organizations frequently underestimate is misuse.

Initially, many enterprise discussions around AI misuse focus on external threats such as malicious prompts, security attacks, or manipulated content. Those risks are important, but operational misuse often emerges internally as well.

Employees may unintentionally expose sensitive information through prompts. Teams may begin using AI-generated outputs without appropriate review processes. Business users may apply AI capabilities beyond the contexts originally approved by governance teams. In some cases, shadow AI adoption spreads faster than official governance structures can respond.

This creates tension inside many organizations.

On one side, leadership teams want to encourage experimentation and innovation. On the other, they recognize that uncontrolled AI usage can introduce compliance, security, reputational, and operational risks very quickly.

Balancing those pressures is not straightforward.

Interestingly, some organizations become so focused on accelerating AI adoption that governance discussions begin only after AI usage has already expanded significantly across teams. By that stage, risk management becomes reactive rather than intentional.

Experienced transformation leaders usually approach this differently. Instead of treating governance as an obstacle to innovation, they position it as an enabler of sustainable adoption. Employees are far more likely to trust and adopt AI systems when clear usage boundaries, accountability models, and oversight mechanisms already exist.

Trust matters more than many organizations initially realize.

Once employees lose confidence in AI-generated outputs, adoption slows rapidly. Similarly, if customers encounter misleading AI behavior or inconsistent responses, reputational damage can emerge much faster than organizations expect.

Trust, once weakened in operational AI systems, is difficult to restore quickly.

This is why Responsible AI leadership is not about eliminating all risk. That is unrealistic. Every technology introduces some level of operational uncertainty. The real objective is ensuring that organizations understand those risks clearly enough to apply AI responsibly, proportionately, and with appropriate oversight.

Figure 3-1 illustrates how hallucinations, bias, misuse, and overreliance can gradually affect enterprise trust when governance and human oversight fail to evolve alongside AI adoption.

Figure 3-1. *Enterprise Risks Emerging from Generative AI Adoption*

Microsoft Responsible AI Principles

As generative AI adoption expands across industries, organizations are increasingly recognizing that technical capability alone is not enough to build trustworthy AI systems. The ability to generate content, automate workflows, or accelerate decision-making may create operational value, but without clear governance and ethical boundaries, those same capabilities can also introduce significant organizational risk.

This is one reason Responsible AI has become a central part of enterprise AI strategy discussions.

While Microsoft's six Responsible AI principles apply to all AI systems, they have become even more important in the era of generative AI. Large language models introduce new considerations such as hallucinations, prompt misuse, grounded responses, content safety, and human oversight. Rather than replacing the existing Responsible AI principles, generative AI reinforces their importance and requires organizations to apply them consistently throughout the AI life cycle.

A common pattern is that many organizations initially approach Responsible AI as a compliance requirement or governance checklist. Over time, however, experienced leaders usually begin viewing it differently. They realize that Responsible AI is fundamentally about maintaining trust, trust from employees, customers, regulators, partners, and leadership teams themselves.

Without trust, AI adoption rarely scales sustainably.

Microsoft's Responsible AI framework reflects this broader perspective. Rather than focusing only on technical safeguards, the framework emphasizes how AI systems should behave operationally within real-world business environments. Microsoft identifies six core Responsible AI principles:

- Fairness
- Reliability and safety
- Privacy and security
- Inclusiveness
- Transparency
- Accountability

While these principles may initially appear conceptual, their operational implications are significant once organizations begin integrating AI into enterprise workflows.

Fairness, for example, extends far beyond avoiding obvious discrimination. In practice, fairness requires organizations to examine whether AI systems produce consistently equitable outcomes across different users, demographics, regions, languages, or operational contexts. This becomes especially important in areas such as recruitment, financial services, healthcare, education, and customer engagement, where biased outcomes may directly affect people's opportunities, experiences, or access to services.

Many organizations discover that fairness challenges are not always immediately visible.

An AI system may perform accurately in one operational environment while producing inconsistent or biased behavior elsewhere because training data, usage patterns, or contextual assumptions differ. This is why Responsible AI cannot rely solely on initial testing. Ongoing monitoring becomes equally important.

Reliability and safety introduce another critical leadership consideration. Enterprise AI systems are increasingly being integrated into operational workflows where inaccurate outputs can influence decisions, customer communication, or business processes directly. As organizations become more dependent on AI-generated content, the consequences of unreliable behavior become harder to ignore.

Reliability in generative AI environments is often less about achieving perfect accuracy and more about understanding operational limitations clearly.

Experienced organizations rarely assume AI outputs are universally correct. Instead, they design workflows where human oversight, validation mechanisms, and escalation processes remain available whenever confidence, context, or risk levels require additional review.

This distinction matters because many failed AI deployments were not caused by technology failure alone. They failed because organizations trusted AI outputs more than their governance maturity justified.

Privacy and security concerns have also become significantly more important as generative AI systems increasingly interact with enterprise data. Employees often use AI tools conversationally and naturally, which creates the risk of sensitive information being shared unintentionally through prompts, uploaded documents, or integrated workflows.

In some organizations, shadow AI usage emerged long before governance teams established formal policies. Employees began using publicly available AI tools independently because they improved productivity immediately. Later, leadership teams realized that confidential business information, customer data, or operational details may already have been exposed outside approved environments.

That situation forced many enterprises to rethink AI governance rapidly.

This is one reason enterprise AI strategies increasingly emphasize grounded AI architectures, secured enterprise environments, role-based access controls, and data protection policies alongside productivity enablement. Responsible AI adoption is no longer viewed as separate from operational security. The two are becoming increasingly interconnected.

Inclusiveness introduces another important dimension that organizations sometimes overlook during early adoption phases.

AI systems should not only function effectively for technically confident users or dominant language groups. Enterprise AI adoption becomes far more sustainable when systems remain accessible across diverse user groups, communication styles, abilities, and operational contexts.

In practice, organizations often discover that adoption barriers are not always technical. Sometimes employees simply do not trust AI systems, feel excluded by interface design, or struggle to understand how AI-generated recommendations are being produced.

That leads directly into the principle of transparency.

One of the more difficult aspects of generative AI is that the systems often appear highly capable while remaining operationally opaque to many users. Employees may not fully understand

- Where information originated
- Why certain responses were generated
- How confidence should be interpreted
- When outputs should be questioned

This creates a subtle but important organizational risk.

When users interact with AI conversationally, the technology can feel authoritative even when uncertainty exists internally within the model itself. Responsible organizations therefore increasingly focus on helping users understand both the capabilities and the limitations of AI-generated outputs rather than encouraging blind trust in automation.

Transparency is becoming especially important in customer-facing environments where organizations may eventually need to explain how AI-assisted decisions or recommendations were produced.

Finally, accountability remains one of the most important principles from a leadership perspective.

As AI systems become integrated into operational decision-making, organizations must remain clear about who is ultimately responsible for outcomes. Generative AI may assist with recommendations, summaries, automation, or analysis, but accountability cannot be delegated entirely to the technology itself.

This becomes particularly important when AI-generated outputs influence hiring decisions, financial recommendations, healthcare guidance, regulatory reporting, or customer communication.

One of the more dangerous misconceptions surrounding AI adoption is the belief that automation somehow reduces organizational responsibility. In reality, widespread AI adoption usually increases the need for governance clarity and leadership accountability rather than reducing it.

Responsible AI leadership therefore requires more than technical awareness. It requires operational discipline, realistic expectations, and an understanding that trust is built gradually through consistent governance, transparency, and responsible usage practices over time.

Figure 3-2 illustrates how Microsoft's Responsible AI principles interact together to support trustworthy and sustainable enterprise AI adoption.

Figure 3-2. *Microsoft Responsible AI Principles in Enterprise Decision-Making*

Trust, Transparency, and Accountability

Some organizations discover this only after employees begin treating AI outputs as safer than they actually are. As organizations integrate generative AI more deeply into everyday operations, technical capability gradually becomes only one part of the broader conversation. Over time, leadership attention usually shifts toward a more difficult question: can the organization trust the AI systems it is beginning to rely on?

That question sounds simple initially. In practice, it becomes surprisingly complicated.

Many enterprise AI systems perform well during demonstrations, pilot projects, or controlled testing environments. The real challenge begins once AI-generated outputs start influencing operational decisions, customer communication, employee workflows, or business recommendations at scale. At that stage, trust is no longer theoretical. It becomes operational.

Interestingly, trust in enterprise AI systems is not created purely through accuracy alone.

Employees may continue trusting systems that occasionally make mistakes if those limitations are understood clearly and governance remains visible. At the same time, even highly capable AI systems can lose organizational trust rapidly if users feel uncertain about how decisions are generated, where information originated, or who remains accountable when problems occur.

This is one reason transparency has become increasingly important in Responsible AI discussions.

Traditional enterprise applications usually operate within predictable workflows. Users understand where information comes from, how rules are applied, and what process generated a particular outcome. Generative AI systems behave differently. Outputs are created dynamically, influenced by prompts, training data, grounding sources, context windows, and probabilistic reasoning patterns that many users never fully see.

As a result, AI systems can appear highly authoritative even when uncertainty exists internally.

That creates an unusual organizational challenge. Employees often assume confidence in the response implies confidence in the accuracy. In reality, generative AI systems may produce fluent and persuasive outputs even when the underlying information is incomplete or incorrect.

This is where transparency becomes operationally important rather than simply ethical.

In many organizations, the issue is not whether employees use AI. The issue is whether they understand when AI-generated outputs should be questioned, validated, or escalated for human review. Responsible AI adoption therefore depends partly on creating realistic expectations around what AI systems can and cannot reliably do.

Interestingly, organizations that communicate AI limitations openly often build stronger long-term trust than organizations that position AI systems as universally reliable. Employees are usually more comfortable adopting AI when they understand its boundaries clearly.

That principle becomes especially important in customer-facing environments.

If organizations deploy AI-assisted systems without sufficient transparency, customers may not realize when they are interacting with AI-generated responses, automated recommendations, or probabilistic decision support systems. Over time, this can create reputational and regulatory concerns, particularly if customers feel misled or unable to challenge incorrect outcomes.

Several emerging AI regulations globally are already placing increased emphasis on explainability, disclosure, and accountability for AI-assisted decisions, particularly in higher-risk industries.

However, transparency alone is not enough.

Organizations must also remain clear about accountability.

One of the more concerning patterns emerging in some enterprise AI deployments is what can be described as "diffused responsibility." As AI systems become more involved in recommendations, summaries, analysis, and operational support, teams sometimes begin assuming the technology itself is responsible for outcomes.

That assumption creates risk very quickly.

AI systems may assist with decisions, but organizational accountability still belongs to people. Employees, managers, operational owners, and leadership teams remain responsible for how AI-generated outputs are used, validated, and governed within business environments.

This distinction becomes critically important in scenarios involving

- Hiring recommendations
- Healthcare guidance

- Financial decisions
- Regulatory reporting
- Customer communication
- Legal documentation

In these situations, the operational consequences of inaccurate or biased outputs can be significant.

Mature organizations therefore design AI-assisted workflows carefully. Instead of removing human responsibility entirely, they clarify where human oversight remains necessary, where escalation paths exist, and where final accountability sits operationally.

In one enterprise environment, a customer support team introduced AI-generated response assistance to accelerate communication handling. Productivity improved quickly, but leadership later discovered that employees were gradually accepting AI-generated responses without sufficient review because the system appeared consistently confident. Eventually, incorrect information reached customers, not because the AI behaved maliciously, but because organizational trust evolved faster than governance controls.

That situation highlighted an important lesson.

Trust in AI systems should grow proportionately with governance maturity, not faster than it.

This balance between trust and oversight is becoming one of the defining leadership challenges in enterprise AI adoption. Too little trust prevents meaningful adoption. Too much trust without governance creates operational risk.

Finding the right balance requires organizational discipline rather than purely technical sophistication.

Another subtle challenge involves explainability.

In many traditional systems, organizations can usually trace decisions through predefined business rules or structured logic. Generative AI systems are often far more difficult to interpret fully, especially when outputs are influenced by large-scale models trained across enormous datasets.

This does not necessarily mean organizations must explain every technical detail to employees or customers. However, leaders increasingly need enough transparency to answer practical operational questions:

- Why was this recommendation generated?
- What information influenced the response?
- How reliable is the output?
- When should human validation occur?
- What safeguards exist if the system behaves unexpectedly?

These questions are becoming increasingly important as AI systems move closer to operational decision-making environments rather than remaining isolated productivity tools.

Interestingly, many enterprises are now realizing that Responsible AI adoption is less about achieving perfect automation and more about designing trustworthy collaboration between humans and AI systems.

That shift matters.

The organizations most likely to scale AI successfully over time are usually not the ones pursuing unrestricted automation aggressively. They are the organizations building operational trust carefully through governance, transparency, accountability, and realistic expectations around AI capability.

Figure 3-3 illustrates how trust in enterprise AI systems emerges through the balance between transparency, human oversight, governance, and accountability rather than through technology capability alone.

Figure 3-3. *Building Trust and Accountability in Enterprise AI Systems*

Regulatory and Compliance Awareness for Leaders

For many organizations, the first phase of generative AI adoption is driven largely by experimentation. Teams explore productivity gains, automate repetitive tasks, and test how AI fits into existing workflows. During this stage, governance conversations often focus mainly on internal policies, acceptable usage guidelines, and operational controls.

Over time, however, the discussion becomes much broader.

As AI systems begin influencing customer interactions, employee decisions, financial processes, healthcare recommendations, or regulated business operations, organizations quickly realize that AI adoption is no longer only an internal technology decision. Regulatory expectations are beginning to evolve alongside the technology itself.

This shift is happening globally.

Governments, regulatory bodies, and industry groups are increasingly examining how organizations use AI systems, particularly in areas involving privacy, fairness, transparency, security, consumer protection, and automated decision-making. While regulations continue evolving, one pattern is already clear: organizations will increasingly be expected to demonstrate not only that AI systems are useful, but also that they are governed responsibly.

Interestingly, many organizations initially assume regulatory concerns apply mainly to highly advanced or autonomous AI systems. In reality, even relatively simple generative AI use cases can introduce compliance implications depending on how the technology interacts with organizational data, customers, employees, or regulated workflows.

For example, a seemingly straightforward AI assistant connected to enterprise documents may still raise questions around

- Data handling
- Information retention
- Confidentiality
- Explainability
- Auditability

Similarly, AI-generated recommendations in recruitment, financial services, healthcare, or legal environments may introduce regulatory scrutiny even when humans remain involved operationally.

This is why experienced transformation leaders rarely treat Responsible AI and compliance as separate conversations.

Operational governance, security, risk management, and regulatory awareness are increasingly interconnected.

One of the more difficult realities for organizations is that regulatory expectations are evolving faster than many traditional governance models were designed to handle. Generative AI systems introduce dynamic behavior, probabilistic outputs, and continuously changing operational contexts, which means organizations cannot always rely on older compliance assumptions designed for deterministic software systems.

That creates uncertainty for leadership teams.

Interestingly, uncertainty itself often becomes a governance challenge. Some organizations delay AI adoption entirely because regulatory expectations appear unclear. Others move too aggressively and only begin considering compliance implications after AI usage has already spread operationally across teams.

Neither extreme tends to work well long term.

Organizations that scale AI successfully usually take a more balanced approach. Instead of waiting for perfect regulatory clarity, they build adaptable governance practices capable of evolving alongside both technology and regulation.

This mindset is becoming increasingly important as global AI regulatory frameworks continue maturing.

The European Union AI Act, for example, introduces a risk-based approach to AI governance, where obligations increase depending on how AI systems are used and the level of potential impact associated with them. High-risk AI systems may require stronger oversight, transparency measures, human accountability, and documentation controls than lower-risk productivity-focused implementations.

Even organizations operating outside the European Union are paying close attention because global enterprises rarely operate within a single regulatory environment anymore.

At the same time, regulatory awareness should not create the impression that AI adoption is becoming impossible or excessively restricted. Most regulatory discussions are not attempting to prevent innovation altogether. The broader objective is usually to ensure that organizations understand the potential consequences of AI deployment and apply appropriate safeguards proportionate to the level of operational risk involved. The difference becomes operationally significant.

Responsible governance is not about eliminating all uncertainty. It is about ensuring organizations remain capable of identifying, assessing, and managing risk realistically as AI adoption expands.

In practice, many enterprise AI risks emerge less from malicious intent and more from operational oversight gaps. Employees may unknowingly expose sensitive information through prompts. AI-generated content may enter regulated workflows without appropriate review. Decision support systems may gradually influence operational behavior beyond their originally intended scope.

These situations often develop incrementally rather than dramatically.

That is one reason strong governance cultures matter so much in enterprise AI adoption. Organizations with mature operational discipline usually adapt to evolving regulatory expectations more effectively because accountability structures, audit processes, security controls, and oversight mechanisms already exist operationally.

Another important leadership consideration involves documentation and explainability.

As AI systems become more integrated into operational environments, organizations may increasingly need to demonstrate

- How AI systems are being used
- What governance controls exist
- Where human oversight remains involved
- How decisions are validated
- How risks are monitored over time

This does not necessarily mean every organization needs highly complex governance structures immediately. In fact, overengineering governance too early can sometimes slow adoption unnecessarily. However, organizations that ignore governance entirely often discover later that scaling AI responsibly becomes much harder once operational dependency has already formed.

In one enterprise discussion involving compliance leaders, executives initially viewed generative AI primarily as a productivity tool rather than a regulated operational capability. Several months later, the organization realized employees were already using AI-generated outputs within customer-facing workflows that required auditability and policy review. Governance discussions that should have happened early became reactive instead.

That situation is becoming increasingly familiar across industries.

The challenge for leadership teams is not simply keeping pace with regulation. It is ensuring that organizational governance maturity evolves alongside AI adoption before operational dependence outpaces oversight capability.

Ultimately, regulatory and compliance awareness in AI leadership is not about becoming legal experts. It is about understanding that enterprise AI systems now operate within broader societal, ethical, operational, and regulatory expectations that organizations can no longer afford to ignore.

Figure 3-4 illustrates how enterprise AI governance increasingly sits at the intersection of innovation, regulation, operational oversight, and organizational accountability.

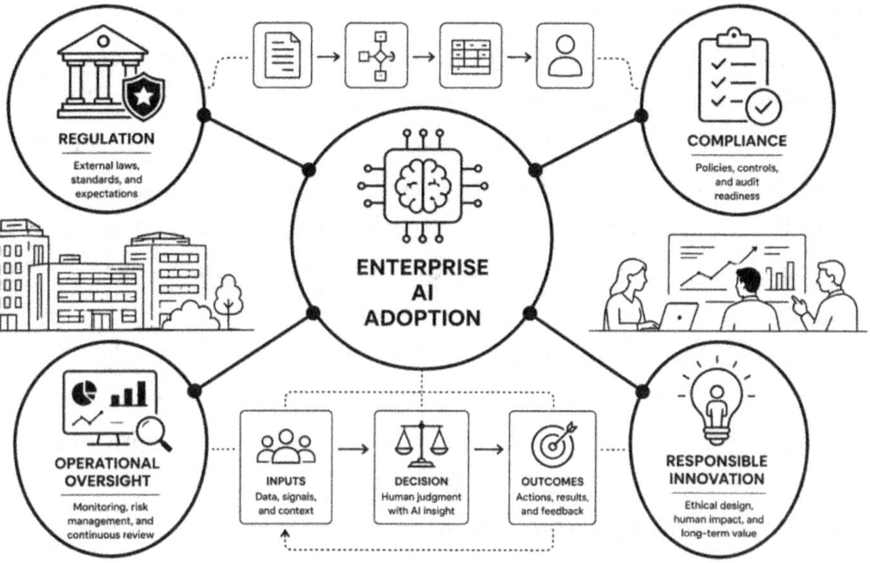

***Figure 3-4.** Regulatory and Governance Considerations in Enterprise AI Adoption*

Risk-Based Decision-Making in AI Adoption

In some organizations, governance discussions happen only after AI usage becomes impossible to track properly. As organizations mature in their AI adoption journey, leadership conversations gradually become less focused on what AI can do and more focused on where AI should be trusted operationally. This shift is important because not every AI use case carries the same level of organizational risk.

Some implementations involve relatively low-impact productivity assistance, such as drafting internal summaries or organizing meeting notes. Others influence customer communication, financial recommendations, healthcare guidance, hiring decisions, or regulatory reporting. The consequences of failure in these environments are very different.

Many enterprise teams eventually realize that applying identical governance models across all AI use cases rarely works effectively.

This is where risk-based decision-making becomes essential.

Rather than treating AI adoption as either completely safe or inherently dangerous, mature organizations evaluate AI initiatives according to the potential impact associated with the workflow, the sensitivity of the data involved, and the operational consequences of inaccurate or inappropriate outputs.

Many organizations initially focus heavily on the technical sophistication of AI systems while underestimating the importance of contextual risk. In practice, a relatively simple AI assistant connected to sensitive business workflows may create greater operational risk than a more advanced system operating within low-impact internal environments.

The surrounding business context matters more than many teams initially expect.

For example, using generative AI to assist employees with internal brainstorming usually introduces manageable operational risk. Using AI-generated recommendations within financial approvals, legal reviews, or healthcare communication introduces a very different level of accountability. The technology itself may appear similar in both situations, but the consequences of error are not.

This is one reason risk-based governance models are becoming increasingly common across enterprise AI strategies.

Instead of applying maximum restrictions universally, organizations begin aligning oversight, validation, transparency, and human review according to the level of operational impact involved. Low-risk use cases may allow broader experimentation and lighter governance. Higher-risk environments generally require stronger oversight, escalation paths, auditability, and human accountability.

That balance is important.

Organizations that introduce excessive governance too early often slow innovation unnecessarily. At the same time, organizations that prioritize speed without understanding operational risk usually encounter governance problems later when AI adoption expands faster than oversight maturity.

Finding the right balance requires judgment rather than rigid rules alone.

In many enterprise environments, AI adoption spreads organically before formal governance structures fully mature. Employees discover productivity benefits quickly and begin integrating AI into daily workflows independently. Initially, this may appear harmless. Over time, however, organizations often realize that unofficial AI usage has already begun influencing operational decisions, customer communication, or sensitive information handling without consistent oversight.

This creates a familiar tension inside many organizations.

Leadership teams want employees to innovate and improve productivity, but they also recognize that unrestricted AI adoption can introduce reputational, compliance, security, and operational risks if governance evolves too slowly.

Experienced transformation leaders rarely respond to this tension by attempting to eliminate experimentation entirely. Instead, they focus on establishing clear boundaries around where AI can be applied safely, where additional oversight becomes necessary, and where human judgment must remain central.

That distinction becomes increasingly important as AI systems move closer to operational decision-making environments.

One of the more subtle risks organizations face is gradual overdependence on AI-generated outputs. This rarely happens intentionally. Employees simply become accustomed to the convenience and speed of AI-assisted workflows. Over time, validation behavior may decline because the system appears consistently reliable. Operational risk often increases gradually rather than through dramatic failure events.

A few inaccurate summaries may initially appear insignificant. A slightly biased recommendation may go unnoticed. An AI-generated response may contain incomplete information without immediately creating visible harm. Yet when these patterns accumulate across workflows, organizational trust, compliance exposure, and decision quality can eventually become affected in ways leadership teams did not anticipate during early adoption phases.

This is why risk-based AI leadership requires continuous evaluation rather than one-time approval processes.

The operational environment surrounding AI systems keeps evolving. New integrations appear, employee behavior changes, regulations mature, and AI capabilities themselves continue advancing rapidly. Governance models therefore need enough flexibility to adapt alongside changing organizational realities.

Another important leadership consideration is proportionality.

Not every AI limitation justifies stopping adoption entirely. Likewise, not every productivity gain justifies accepting uncontrolled operational risk. Mature organizations usually avoid both extremes. They recognize that Responsible AI adoption involves making informed trade-offs rather than pursuing either unrestricted automation or excessive caution.

In practice, many successful enterprise AI strategies evolve progressively.

Organizations often begin with lower-risk internal productivity use cases where governance maturity can develop gradually alongside adoption experience. As operational confidence improves and oversight capabilities mature, broader or higher-impact AI use cases may eventually become appropriate.

This staged approach tends to create stronger long-term sustainability because organizational learning develops alongside technological integration.

What many organizations eventually realize is that some of the most successful enterprise AI programs are not necessarily the fastest-moving ones. They are often the organizations that maintain enough operational discipline to scale AI responsibly without losing employee trust, governance clarity, or accountability along the way.

That discipline becomes especially important when leadership teams evaluate trade-offs between innovation speed and operational safety.

AB-731 reflects this mindset repeatedly. The exam rarely rewards decisions based purely on technological ambition. Instead, it consistently favors balanced judgment where business value, governance maturity, operational readiness, and proportional risk management remain aligned together.

Ultimately, risk-based decision-making in AI adoption is less about avoiding uncertainty entirely and more about ensuring organizations understand where uncertainty exists, how significant the consequences may become, and what level of oversight remains appropriate as AI adoption expands over time.

Figure 3-5 illustrates how enterprise AI governance becomes progressively stronger as organizational risk, operational impact, and oversight requirements increase together.

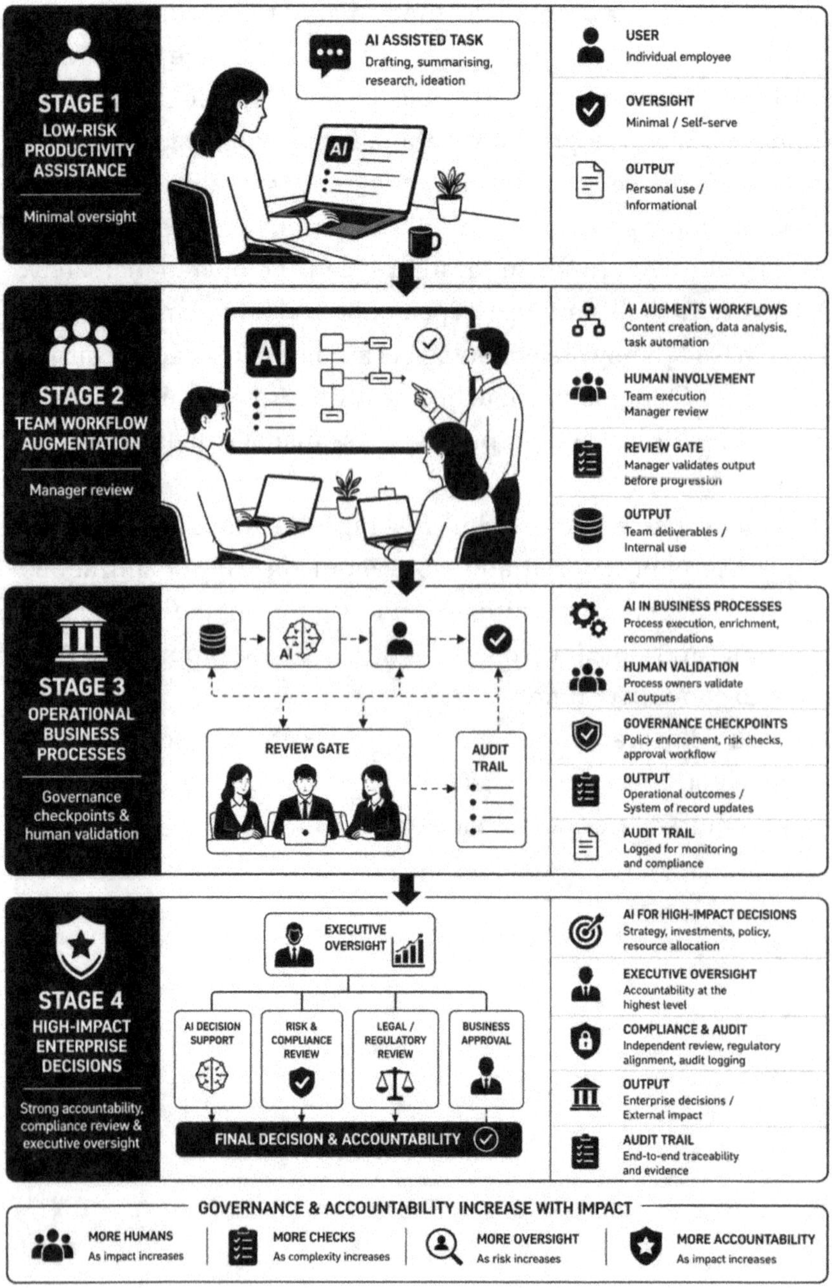

Figure 3-5. *Risk-Based Governance in Enterprise AI Adoption*

Leader's Lens

One of the more interesting patterns emerging across enterprise AI adoption is that organizations often spend significant time evaluating whether AI systems are technically capable, but far less time evaluating whether the organization itself is operationally prepared to use them responsibly.

In reality, most enterprise AI failures do not begin as technology failures. They usually emerge from gaps in governance, oversight, accountability, or unrealistic assumptions about how employees will interact with AI-generated outputs in everyday workflows.

Trust plays a central role here.

Employees may initially embrace AI systems enthusiastically because the productivity benefits are visible immediately. However, trust can decline surprisingly quickly if systems produce misleading information, behave inconsistently, or operate without clear accountability boundaries. Once confidence weakens, adoption becomes far harder to sustain.

Experienced transformation leaders therefore approach Responsible AI differently from traditional compliance exercises. Instead of treating governance as a barrier to innovation, they recognize that strong governance is often what allows innovation to scale safely over time.

Interestingly, the organizations creating the most sustainable AI value are not always the fastest adopters. They are usually the organizations disciplined enough to balance innovation speed with operational trust, human oversight, and governance maturity as adoption expands.

Exam Catch

One of the most common mistakes candidates make in AB-731-style scenarios is assuming that Responsible AI means slowing innovation as much as possible or introducing maximum governance controls immediately.

In practice, Microsoft's leadership-focused approach to Responsible AI is far more balanced.

The exam rarely rewards answers based on extreme positions such as

- Removing human oversight entirely
- Blocking AI adoption because some risk exists
- Introducing excessive governance that prevents practical adoption altogether

Instead, AB-731 consistently favors decisions that align governance with the level of operational risk involved.

For example, lower-risk productivity use cases may support broader experimentation with lighter oversight, while higher-risk environments involving customer impact, financial decisions, regulated data, or operational accountability generally require stronger governance, validation, and human review processes.

The TRUST Lens for Responsible AI Decision-Making

As organizations expand AI adoption across business functions, one of the more difficult leadership challenges is determining how much governance is appropriate for a particular AI use case. Some environments require extensive oversight and accountability controls, while others allow greater flexibility for experimentation and operational learning.

In practice, operationally disciplined organizations rarely evaluate AI decisions through technology capability alone. They also examine how the system affects trust, operational risk, employee behavior, and accountability over time.

One useful way to approach this is through the TRUST Lens, a simple leadership framework for evaluating AI adoption decisions in enterprise environments.

The first element is Transparency. Organizations should understand how AI systems are being used, where information originates, and when employees or customers are interacting with AI-generated outputs. Lack of transparency often creates misplaced confidence and weakens organizational trust over time.

The second element is Risk Awareness. Not every AI use case carries the same consequences. Leaders should evaluate the operational, reputational, regulatory, and customer impact associated with inaccurate or inappropriate outputs before scaling adoption broadly.

The third element is User Impact. Responsible AI decisions should consider how employees, customers, and stakeholders experience the system operationally. AI systems that create confusion, inconsistency, exclusion, or overdependence often struggle to maintain trust even when technically capable.

The fourth element is Security and Compliance. As generative AI systems interact increasingly with enterprise data and operational workflows, organizations must ensure that governance, access control, privacy protection, and compliance expectations evolve alongside adoption.

The final element is Traceability and Accountability. Organizations should remain clear about who is responsible for AI-assisted outcomes, where human oversight remains necessary, and how decisions can be reviewed or escalated when required.

The TRUST Lens is not designed to slow innovation. Its purpose is to help organizations scale AI adoption more sustainably by ensuring that operational trust evolves alongside technological capability.

In many enterprise environments, AI adoption accelerates much faster than governance maturity. Frameworks such as TRUST help leadership teams evaluate whether organizational readiness is keeping pace with operational dependency on AI systems.

Figure 3-6 illustrates how the TRUST Lens helps organizations balance innovation, governance, accountability, and operational trust when evaluating enterprise AI adoption decisions.

Figure 3-6. *The TRUST Lens for Responsible AI Leadership*

Summary

This chapter explored one of the most important realities of enterprise AI adoption: the moment AI systems begin influencing operational decisions, customer interactions, or business workflows, the conversation expands far beyond technology capability alone.

In the early stages of generative AI adoption, organizations often focus heavily on opportunity, productivity, and innovation. Over time, however, attention shifts toward a more difficult set of questions. Can AI-generated outputs be trusted consistently? How should organizations manage hallucinations, bias, misuse, and operational overdependence? Where should human oversight remain involved? And how much governance is appropriate without slowing innovation unnecessarily?

These questions are no longer theoretical.

As AI systems become embedded within enterprise workflows, trust gradually becomes one of the most important factors influencing long-term adoption success. Employees may initially embrace AI systems enthusiastically because the productivity benefits are immediate and visible. Yet trust can weaken surprisingly quickly if AI-generated outputs become misleading, inconsistent, opaque, or operationally unreliable.

This is one reason Responsible AI is becoming increasingly central to enterprise leadership discussions.

The chapter examined Microsoft's Responsible AI principles and explored how fairness, reliability, transparency, inclusiveness, privacy, security, and accountability influence enterprise AI adoption in practical environments. Importantly, Responsible AI was positioned not as a compliance exercise alone, but as a broader organizational discipline designed to support sustainable and trustworthy AI adoption over time.

Another major theme throughout the chapter was the importance of proportional governance.

Not every AI use case carries the same level of operational risk. Lower-risk productivity workflows may support broader experimentation and lighter oversight, while higher-impact environments involving financial decisions, healthcare guidance, customer communication, or regulated data generally require stronger governance, human validation, and accountability structures.

Mature organizations eventually realize that Responsible AI is not about eliminating uncertainty entirely. That is unrealistic. The goal is to understand where uncertainty exists, what consequences may emerge, and how governance maturity should evolve alongside operational AI dependency.

Over time, many enterprise AI failures do not begin as technical failures. They emerge gradually through weak oversight, misplaced trust, unclear accountability, or governance structures that fail to keep pace with adoption. In many cases, organizations only recognize the importance of Responsible AI after AI systems have already become operationally influential.

This chapter also highlighted the growing importance of regulatory and compliance awareness. As AI adoption expands globally, organizations are increasingly expected to demonstrate that AI systems are governed responsibly, transparently, and proportionately according to the level of operational impact involved.

Taken together, this chapter reinforces an important leadership mindset that appears repeatedly throughout AB-731: successful AI transformation is not defined solely by how quickly organizations adopt AI technologies. It is equally defined by how responsibly, transparently, and sustainably those technologies are governed once they become operationally real.

As the next chapter begins exploring Microsoft Copilot, Copilot Studio, and Azure AI capabilities, this leadership perspective becomes increasingly important. Selecting the right AI solution is not only about understanding product features or technical capability. Organizations must also evaluate how these platforms align with business goals, operational readiness, governance expectations, and real-world enterprise scenarios. The ability to position AI solutions responsibly and strategically is what ultimately separates experimentation from sustainable business adoption.

The illustration in Figure 3-7 summarizes how Responsible AI leadership depends on balancing innovation, governance, human oversight, and organizational trust together rather than treating them as separate priorities.

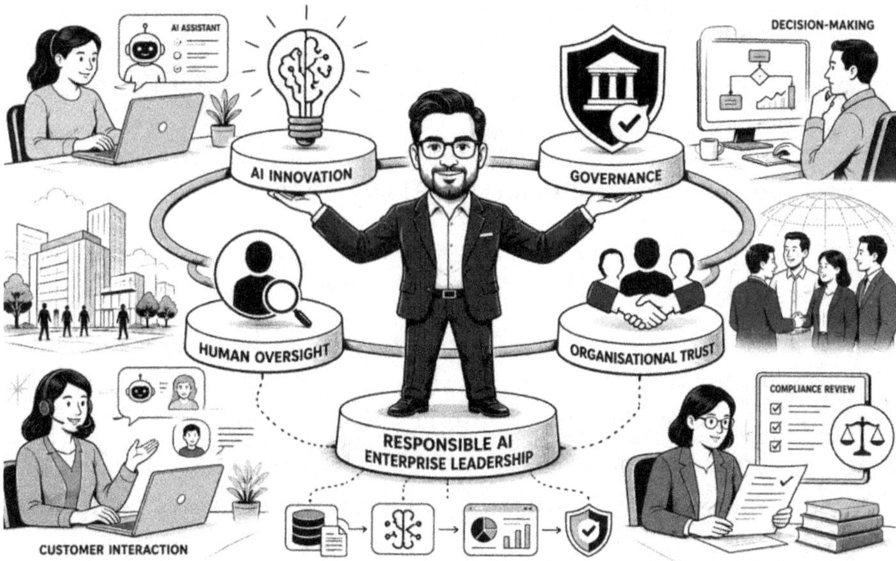

Figure 3-7. *Responsible AI Leadership: Balancing Innovation, Governance, and Trust*

Exam-Style Questions

Question 1

A company introduces generative AI assistants to help employees prepare internal reports and customer communication drafts. After a few months, managers notice that employees are increasingly accepting AI-generated responses without reviewing them carefully.

What is the biggest concern in this situation?

A. Employees are not using AI frequently enough

B. Employees are beginning to rely on AI outputs more than the organization's review processes can support

C. AI systems should immediately replace all manual communication workflows

D. The organization should stop AI adoption completely

Correct Answer

B

Explanation

One of the most common operational risks in generative AI adoption is gradual overreliance on AI-generated outputs. Productivity may improve quickly, but governance and validation processes must evolve alongside adoption.

Question 2

A healthcare organization wants to use generative AI to support patient communication workflows. Leadership teams are concerned about inaccurate outputs and the impact they could have on patient trust.

What is the most appropriate leadership response?

A. Remove human oversight completely to improve efficiency

B. Restrict AI usage permanently to technical departments only

C. Introduce governance controls, validation processes, and clear accountability

D. Delay all AI adoption indefinitely because hallucinations exist

Correct Answer

C

Explanation

In higher-risk environments, organizations usually need stronger oversight, governance, and accountability structures. Responsible AI leadership focuses on balancing innovation with operational trust and patient safety.

Question 3

A leadership team believes every AI initiative should immediately follow the strictest possible governance controls to minimize organizational risk.

Why might this approach create problems?

A. Strong governance is unnecessary for enterprise AI adoption

B. Too many restrictions too early may discourage practical experimentation

C. Employees should manage AI governance independently

D. Governance only becomes important after AI systems scale globally

Correct Answer

B

Explanation

Responsible AI does not mean applying maximum restrictions everywhere. Mature organizations usually align governance according to operational risk, business context, and organizational readiness.

Question 4

An organization deploys AI-assisted customer support systems without clearly informing customers when responses are AI-generated.

Which Responsible AI principle is most directly affected?

A. Transparency

B. Infrastructure optimization

C. Workflow automation

D. Scalability

Correct Answer

A

Explanation

Customers should understand when AI-generated systems are influencing communication or recommendations. Transparency helps maintain trust and supports Responsible AI adoption.

Question 5

A financial services company uses AI-generated recommendations to support internal analysts. Employees still make final decisions, but teams are becoming unclear about who is ultimately responsible for validating the outputs.

What is the greatest organizational risk in this scenario?

A. AI systems are improving productivity too quickly

B. Employees may stop using AI systems entirely

C. Teams may stop being clear about who is actually responsible for decisions

D. The organization lacks advanced AI infrastructure

Correct Answer

C

Explanation

As AI systems become integrated into operational workflows, organizations must remain clear about accountability boundaries. AI may assist decisions, but responsibility still belongs to people.

Question 6

A company launches several AI productivity initiatives successfully, but governance discussions only begin after AI usage expands significantly across departments.

What does this situation most likely indicate?

A. The organization focused on speed before governance maturity was fully established

B. Employees are resisting AI adoption completely

C. Governance is no longer necessary once AI tools become operational

D. AI adoption should stop immediately across all departments

Correct Answer

A

Explanation

Many organizations initially prioritize experimentation and operational speed, only later realizing that governance structures have not evolved at the same pace as adoption.

Question 7

During internal testing, an enterprise AI assistant produces responses that sound highly professional and convincing, but some information later turns out to be inaccurate.

What risk does this situation best represent?

A. Cloud infrastructure limitations

B. Employees are trusting confident AI responses without verifying accuracy properly

C. Insufficient workflow automation capability

D. AI systems are becoming technically outdated

Correct Answer

B

Explanation

One of the most difficult aspects of generative AI is that inaccurate information can still appear highly credible. This increases the risk of misplaced trust and reduced human validation.

Question 8

A leadership team is deciding whether a low-risk internal productivity tool requires the same level of governance as an AI system involved in regulatory reporting.

What is the most appropriate approach?

A. Apply identical governance controls across every AI system

B. Avoid governance entirely for internal productivity tools

C. Apply governance according to how much operational impact the AI system could create

D. Delay all AI projects until global AI regulations become fully standardized

Correct Answer

C

Explanation

Responsible AI governance should remain proportionate to operational risk, customer impact, compliance exposure, and organizational context rather than applying identical controls everywhere.

Question 9

Employees across different departments begin using publicly available AI tools independently without formal oversight, usage policies, or security guidance from leadership.

What organizational issue is most likely developing?

A. AI productivity improvements are becoming difficult to measure

B. AI adoption is spreading faster than governance and oversight structures

C. Employees are avoiding experimentation with AI systems

D. Enterprise AI systems are becoming less accessible technically

Correct Answer

B

Explanation

This situation reflects a common enterprise pattern where AI adoption expands organically before governance, security, and operational policies are fully established.

Question 10

An executive team asks whether Responsible AI should mainly be handled by technical engineering teams because the challenges are primarily technical.

What is the best leadership response?

A. Responsible AI is mainly a model-training issue for technical teams

B. Responsible AI is primarily a legal issue unrelated to operations

C. Responsible AI is an organizational responsibility involving governance, trust, accountability, and operational oversight

D. Responsible AI only becomes important after large-scale AI transformation occurs

Correct Answer

C

Explanation

AB-731 consistently frames Responsible AI as a broader organizational leadership responsibility rather than a purely technical concern. Sustainable AI adoption depends on governance, accountability, transparency, and operational trust working together.

CHAPTER 4

Microsoft Copilot and Microsoft Foundry Capabilities

Introduction

As organizations move beyond experimenting with generative AI, a new challenge begins to emerge. The question is no longer whether AI can create value. Most leadership teams have already seen enough evidence to believe that it can.

The more difficult question is deciding where to start.

Over the past few years, Microsoft's AI portfolio has expanded significantly. Organizations can now improve employee productivity with Microsoft 365 Copilot, build conversational experiences through Copilot Studio, and develop custom AI solutions using Microsoft Foundry and related AI services. Each option offers distinct capabilities, different implementation approaches, and varying levels of flexibility.

For business leaders, this creates both opportunity and confusion.

In many executive discussions, the first instinct is often to search for a single AI platform that can solve every problem. In reality, enterprise AI adoption rarely works that way. Different business challenges require different approaches. A solution designed to help employees work more

K. Shaikh, *Microsoft Certified: AI Transformation Leader Study Companion*, Certification Study Companion Series, https://doi.org/10.1007/979-8-8688-3168-3_4

efficiently within familiar Microsoft 365 applications serves a different purpose from a custom AI application connected to enterprise data and business processes.

This is one reason AI solution selection has become an increasingly important leadership responsibility.

Choosing the wrong solution may not result in technical failure. More commonly, it leads to unnecessary complexity, delayed adoption, higher costs, or unrealized business value. Organizations sometimes invest significant effort building custom solutions when an existing Copilot capability would have been sufficient. Others begin with productivity tools only to discover that their requirements demand greater customization and control.

The most successful organizations approach this differently. Rather than starting with technology, they begin with the business problem they are trying to solve. They evaluate who will use the solution, what outcomes are expected, how much flexibility is required, and how the solution will fit within existing workflows.

This chapter examines Microsoft's AI ecosystem from that perspective. It explores the role of Microsoft 365 Copilot, Copilot Studio, and Microsoft Foundry, not as isolated products but as capabilities that address different organizational needs and levels of AI maturity.

Before exploring each in detail, it is useful to understand how these offerings fit within the broader Microsoft AI ecosystem. Figure 4-1 provides a high-level view of where Microsoft 365 Copilot, Copilot Studio, and Microsoft Foundry typically sit within an enterprise AI strategy and the types of business challenges they are designed to address.

The goal is not to memorize product features. It is to develop the judgment needed to recognize which Microsoft AI capability is most appropriate for a given business scenario. That mindset appears repeatedly throughout AB-731 and reflects the way successful AI adoption decisions are made in practice.

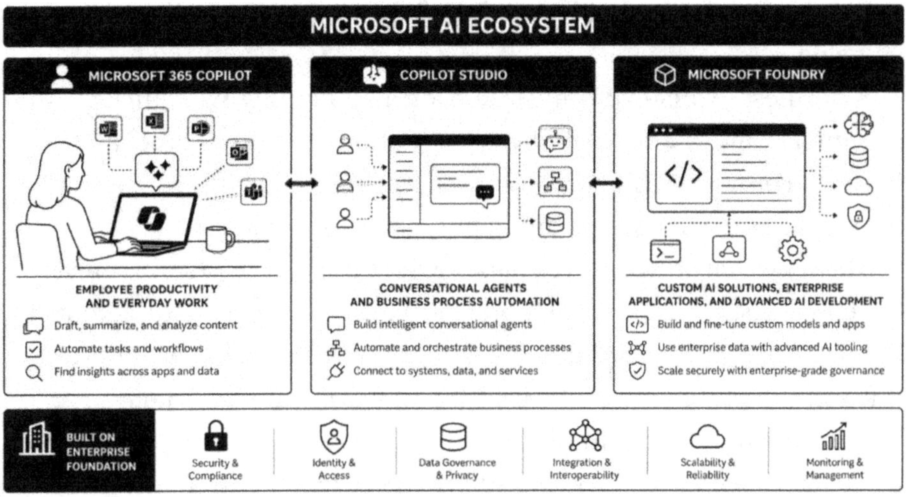

***Figure 4-1.** The Microsoft AI Ecosystem at a Glance*

The Microsoft AI ecosystem extends beyond the capabilities discussed in this chapter and includes services such as Azure AI Services, Azure AI Search, and other platform components that support intelligent applications.

Many of these capabilities are available through or alongside Microsoft Foundry. However, for AI Transformation Leaders preparing for AB-731, the primary focus is understanding when to use Microsoft 365 Copilot, Copilot Studio, and Microsoft Foundry to address different business scenarios.

Understanding the Microsoft AI Ecosystem

Many organizations begin their AI journey assuming they need to select a single platform that will address every requirement. In practice, enterprise AI adoption rarely follows such a straightforward path. Different business challenges require different capabilities, levels of customization, and implementation approaches.

This is one reason the Microsoft AI ecosystem can initially appear confusing.

A business leader exploring Microsoft's AI offerings will quickly encounter names such as Microsoft 365 Copilot, Copilot Studio, and Microsoft Foundry. While these solutions share a common AI foundation, they are designed to address different organizational needs.

The confusion often arises because all three can appear to solve similar problems at first glance. Each supports conversational experiences, automation, information retrieval, and AI-assisted decision-making. However, the level of flexibility, customization, and business ownership differs significantly.

Consider a simple example.

An employee who wants help summarizing emails, drafting documents, or preparing meeting notes does not typically require a custom AI application. The goal is productivity within familiar business tools. In that situation, Microsoft 365 Copilot is often the most natural starting point because it operates within applications employees already use every day.

Now consider a different scenario.

A customer service team wants an AI assistant capable of answering policy questions, guiding users through processes, and integrating with business workflows. The organization may need greater control over conversations, actions, and user experiences. In this situation, Copilot Studio may be more appropriate because it enables organizations to create tailored conversational experiences without requiring extensive software development.

The requirements change again when organizations need AI solutions that extend beyond predefined productivity or conversational scenarios.

A business may want to build a custom application that combines enterprise data, retrieval systems, large language models, governance controls, and specialized business logic. These requirements often lead organizations toward Microsoft Foundry, where AI capabilities can be designed, developed, and integrated according to specific organizational needs.

What many leadership teams eventually discover is that these offerings are not competing solutions. They are complementary capabilities that address different layers of enterprise AI adoption.

Some organizations begin with Microsoft 365 Copilot and later introduce Copilot Studio to support customer-facing interactions. Others use Microsoft Foundry to build specialized AI applications while simultaneously enabling employee productivity through Microsoft 365 Copilot. As AI maturity increases, multiple capabilities often coexist within the same organization

This is why solution selection should begin with the business problem rather than the technology itself.

The most effective AI adoption decisions usually start by understanding

- Who the users are
- What outcome is required
- How much customization is needed
- Where the solution will operate
- How it will fit within existing business processes

Figure 4-2 illustrates how Microsoft 365 Copilot, Copilot Studio, and Microsoft Foundry occupy different positions within the broader enterprise AI landscape while supporting complementary business objectives.

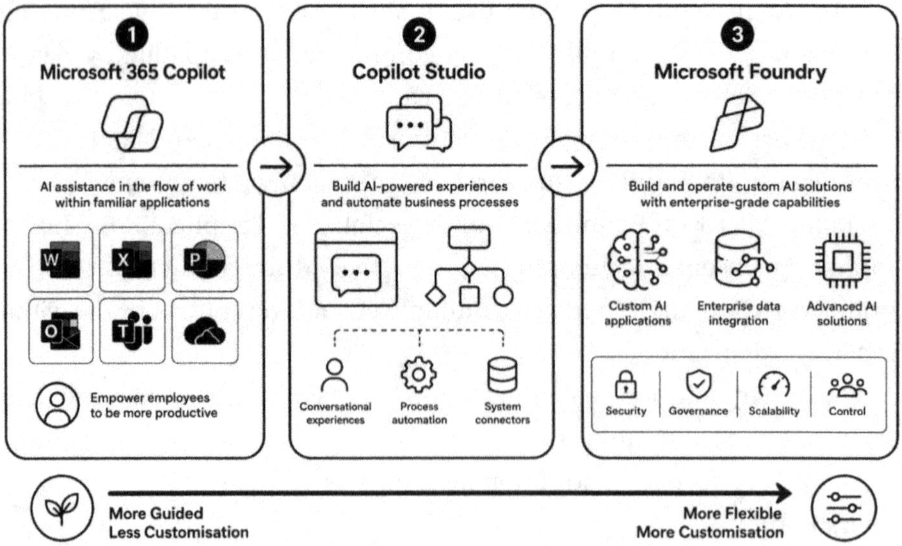

***Figure 4-2.** Positioning Microsoft AI Capabilities Across Enterprise Needs*

Microsoft 365 Copilot

As shown in Figure 4-3, Microsoft 365 Copilot brings AI assistance directly into familiar Microsoft 365 experiences, supporting employees across everyday productivity activities.

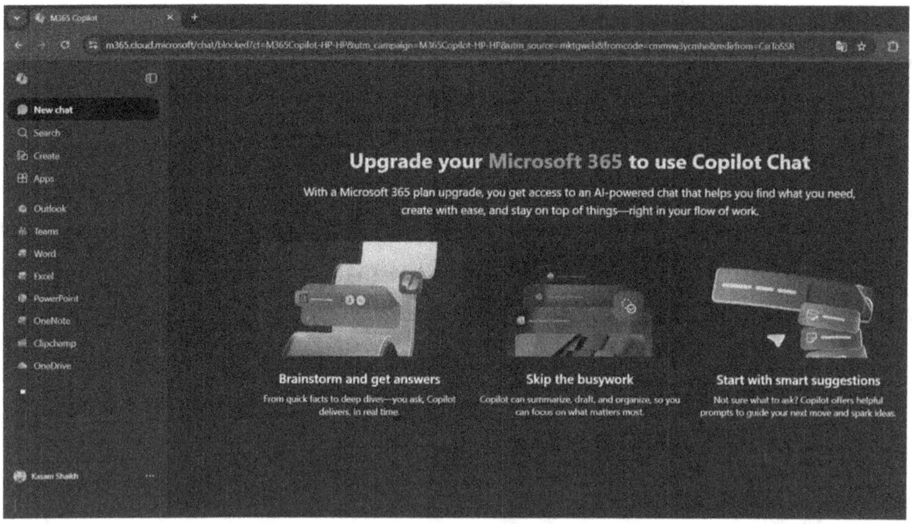

Figure 4-3. *Microsoft 365 Copilot Home Experience*

When generative AI first entered mainstream business discussions, many organizations immediately began exploring how it could improve employee productivity. The logic was straightforward. Most employees spend a significant portion of their day reading emails, attending meetings, searching for information, creating documents, preparing presentations, or responding to requests. Even small improvements in these activities could create meaningful organizational value when applied at scale.

This is the problem Microsoft 365 Copilot was designed to address.

Rather than introducing an entirely new application that employees must learn and adopt, Microsoft 365 Copilot brings AI capabilities into tools that many organizations already use every day. Employees can interact with AI within familiar applications such as Word, Excel, PowerPoint, Outlook, Teams, and other Microsoft 365 experiences.

From a leadership perspective, this distinction is important.

One of the most common barriers to technology adoption is behavioral change. Employees are often asked to learn new systems, navigate unfamiliar interfaces, and modify established ways of working. Microsoft

365 Copilot takes a different approach by embedding AI within existing workflows. Instead of asking employees to change where they work, it enhances how they work within tools they already know.

This often makes adoption easier.

Consider a manager preparing a project update for senior leadership. Traditionally, this may involve reviewing meeting notes, searching through emails, gathering supporting information, and manually drafting a report. With Microsoft 365 Copilot, much of this effort can be accelerated through AI-assisted summarization, content generation, and information retrieval.

The value is not that the AI performs the entire task independently. The value comes from reducing the time employees spend on repetitive activities so they can focus more attention on judgment, decision-making, and business outcomes.

This distinction is sometimes overlooked during AI strategy discussions.

Many organizations initially evaluate AI based on how much work can be automated. In practice, some of the most immediate benefits come from augmentation rather than automation. Employees remain responsible for decisions and outputs, but AI helps them complete tasks more efficiently.

This is one reason Microsoft 365 Copilot is often viewed as an entry point into enterprise AI adoption.

The implementation effort is generally lower than building custom AI applications. Users interact with AI through familiar business applications. Governance and security controls can align with existing Microsoft 365 environments. Most importantly, the business value is relatively easy to explain because employees experience the benefits directly in their daily work.

That said, Microsoft 365 Copilot is not intended to solve every AI challenge.

A common mistake is assuming that because Copilot improves productivity, it can also address highly specialized business requirements. Organizations occasionally attempt to use Microsoft 365 Copilot for scenarios that require custom workflows, unique business logic, specialized data integrations, or tailored customer experiences.

These situations typically require a different approach.

Microsoft 365 Copilot is strongest when the objective is improving how employees work within the Microsoft 365 ecosystem. It excels at helping users create, analyze, summarize, organize, and communicate information more effectively. When requirements move beyond productivity enhancement and into custom application development or specialized business processes, other Microsoft AI capabilities may become more appropriate.

This is why successful AI adoption begins with understanding the nature of the problem being solved.

If the primary objective is to help employees become more productive within the tools they already use, Microsoft 365 Copilot is often a natural starting point. If the objective is to build entirely new AI-powered experiences, organizations may need to look beyond productivity-focused solutions.

Figure 4-4 illustrates how Microsoft 365 Copilot integrates into everyday business workflows and where it creates value across common employee activities.

Figure 4-4. *Microsoft 365 Copilot in Everyday Workflows*

Copilot Studio

While Microsoft 365 Copilot focuses on helping employees become more productive within familiar business applications, organizations often encounter a different requirement as their AI journey progresses.

The conversation shifts from

"How can AI help our employees work more efficiently?"

to

"How can we create AI-powered experiences for employees, customers, partners, or citizens?"

This is where Copilot Studio enters the picture. Figure 4-5 provides a view of the Copilot Studio environment, illustrating the platform through which organisations can create and manage tailored conversational AI experiences.

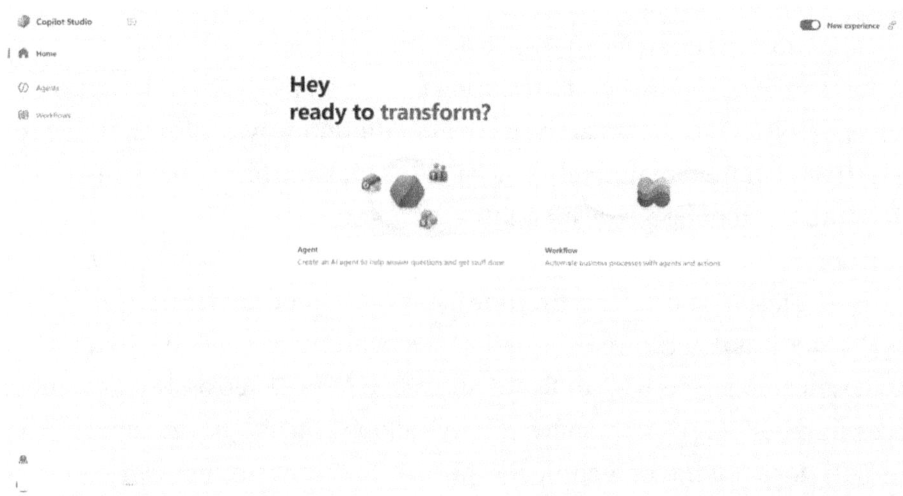

***Figure 4-5.** Copilot Studio Home Experience*

Many organizations eventually identify business processes that involve repetitive questions, routine interactions, information requests, or simple decision pathways. Service desks answer the same questions repeatedly. Human resources teams respond to common policy enquiries. Customer support centers handle large volumes of routine requests that follow predictable patterns.

These situations are often less about productivity and more about accessibility.

People need information quickly. They need guidance through processes. They need answers without waiting for a person to become available.

Historically, organizations addressed these requirements through chatbots, knowledge bases, web forms, or self-service portals. While these approaches provided value, they often required users to navigate predefined menus, search through large amounts of content, or follow rigid interaction paths.

Generative AI changes that experience.

Instead of navigating systems, users can engage in natural language conversations. Questions can be asked in different ways. Information can be retrieved more dynamically. Interactions feel less like using software and more like having a conversation.

Copilot Studio enables organizations to create these experiences.

From a leadership perspective, one of the most important aspects of Copilot Studio is that it lowers the barrier to creating conversational solutions. Business teams can design, configure, and refine AI-powered assistants without necessarily building custom software applications from the ground up.

This does not mean technical expertise becomes unnecessary. More advanced scenarios still require integration, governance, security controls, and operational oversight. However, the platform enables organizations to move more quickly when the objective is creating tailored conversational experiences rather than developing entirely custom AI applications.

Consider a common example.

A large organization may have thousands of employees spread across multiple locations. Questions about leave policies, travel guidelines, onboarding procedures, training programs, or benefits are asked repeatedly throughout the year. Traditionally, these enquiries create workload for HR teams while employees spend time searching for information.

A Copilot created through Copilot Studio can provide a conversational interface that helps employees locate information, navigate policies, and complete routine tasks more efficiently.

The same principle applies externally.

Customers may need assistance understanding products, tracking requests, accessing services, or finding information. Rather than relying entirely on traditional support channels, organizations can create AI-powered assistants that provide guidance while maintaining appropriate governance and escalation paths.

This highlights an important distinction between Microsoft 365 Copilot and Copilot Studio.

Microsoft 365 Copilot primarily enhances individual productivity within existing Microsoft 365 workflows.

Copilot Studio focuses on creating AI experiences that other people interact with.

The users, objectives, and business outcomes are different.

One supports employees performing their daily work. The other enables organizations to design conversational experiences that extend across business processes, departments, and customer interactions.

That said, organizations should avoid assuming that every conversational requirement automatically needs a custom copilot.

A common mistake is introducing unnecessary complexity for relatively straightforward needs. Sometimes a productivity-focused solution is sufficient. In other situations, organizations may require capabilities that extend beyond conversational experiences entirely and move toward custom AI applications integrated with enterprise systems and specialized business logic.

These scenarios often lead to the next layer of Microsoft's AI ecosystem: Microsoft Foundry.

Before exploring that capability, it is important to understand that Copilot Studio occupies a unique position within enterprise AI adoption. It bridges the gap between productivity-focused AI and fully customized AI development, enabling organizations to create tailored experiences without necessarily building everything from scratch.

Figure 4-6 illustrates how Copilot Studio enables organizations to create conversational experiences across employees, customers, and business processes while maintaining governance and operational control.

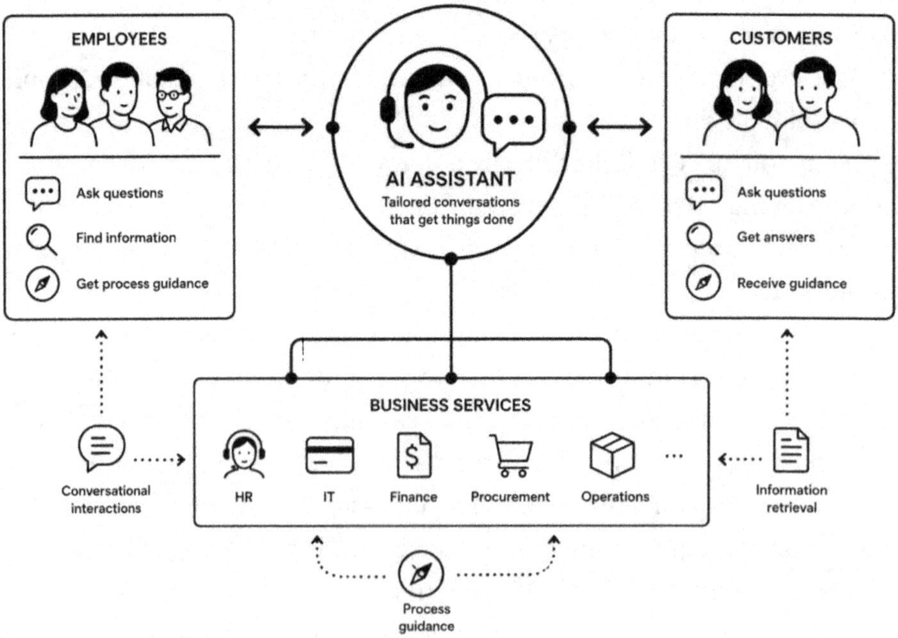

Figure 4-6. *Copilot Studio as a Bridge Between Productivity and Business Processes*

Microsoft Foundry and Custom AI Solutions

As organizations become more confident in their use of AI, the nature of their requirements often begins to change.

Initially, the focus is usually on productivity. Employees want help drafting documents, summarizing meetings, analyzing information, and completing routine tasks more efficiently. Microsoft 365 Copilot is often well suited to these scenarios because it integrates directly into everyday work.

Over time, however, organizations start asking different questions.

They may want to create AI solutions that understand specialized business processes, interact with enterprise systems, retrieve information from multiple sources, or support unique customer experiences. The objective is no longer simply to improve how employees work. Instead, the organization is seeking to create new capabilities that did not previously exist.

At some point, organizations encounter requirements that cannot be addressed through productivity tools or conversational experiences alone. They need AI solutions designed around their own data, processes, and competitive differentiators. This is where Microsoft Foundry becomes relevant. As shown in Figure 4-7, Microsoft Foundry provides an environment for organisations to design, build, and manage customised AI solutions according to their business requirements.

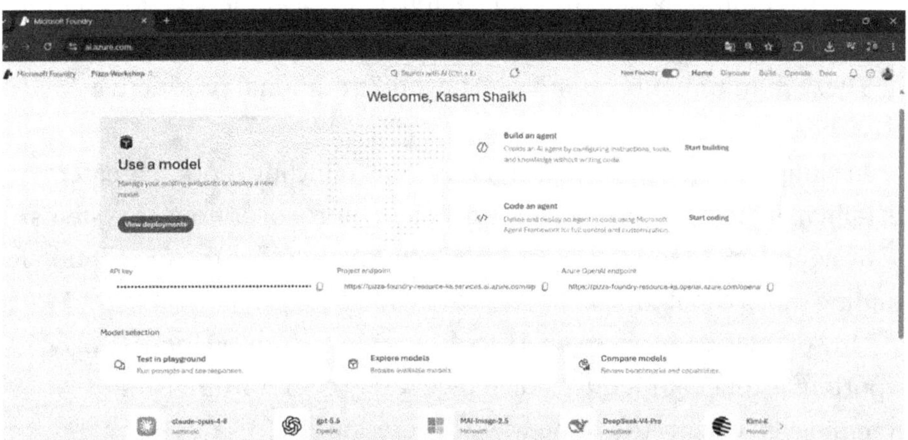

***Figure 4-7.** Microsoft Foundry Home Experience*

Unlike Microsoft 365 Copilot or Copilot Studio, which focus on predefined productivity and conversational experiences, Microsoft Foundry provides a platform for designing, building, and managing custom AI solutions. It enables organizations to combine AI models, enterprise data, retrieval systems, orchestration capabilities, governance controls, and application logic into solutions tailored to their specific needs.

From a leadership perspective, the distinction is significant.

The question is no longer:

"How can AI assist users?"

Instead, it becomes:

"How can AI become part of the business process itself?"

Consider a financial services organization that wants to analyze large volumes of regulatory documentation and provide recommendations to compliance teams. The solution may need to retrieve information from internal repositories, apply business-specific rules, maintain auditability, and integrate with existing operational systems.

Similarly, a healthcare provider may want an AI-powered assistant capable of combining patient information, clinical guidance, operational procedures, and organizational policies within a governed environment.

These requirements extend well beyond traditional productivity assistance.

In situations such as these, organizations typically require greater flexibility, deeper integration, and stronger control over how AI systems are designed and operated. Microsoft Foundry provides the foundation for building those capabilities.

One of the reasons custom AI solutions are becoming increasingly important is that competitive advantage rarely comes from using technology in exactly the same way as everyone else.

Many organizations can benefit from productivity tools. Many can deploy conversational assistants. The real differentiation often emerges when AI is applied to unique business processes, specialized knowledge, proprietary data, or industry-specific challenges.

This does not mean every organization should immediately pursue custom AI development.

In fact, one of the more common mistakes made during AI adoption is introducing unnecessary complexity too early. Some organizations become so focused on building sophisticated AI solutions that they overlook opportunities to create value using existing capabilities.

A useful principle is to begin with the business problem rather than the technology.

If the requirement can be addressed effectively through Microsoft 365 Copilot, there may be little reason to build a custom solution. If the goal is creating a tailored conversational experience, Copilot Studio may be sufficient. Microsoft Foundry becomes most relevant when the organization requires a level of flexibility, integration, or customization that cannot be achieved through productivity-focused or conversational platforms alone.

Another important consideration is ownership.

Custom AI solutions typically involve broader organizational participation than productivity deployments. Business stakeholders, architects, developers, security teams, governance functions, and operational owners often need to collaborate throughout the life cycle of the solution.

As a result, successful custom AI initiatives are rarely technology projects alone. They are business transformation initiatives supported by technology.

This distinction appears frequently in AI transformation programs. Organizations that view custom AI purely as a technical implementation often struggle to realize expected value. Those that align AI development with business objectives, operational processes, and measurable outcomes are generally more successful.

For leaders, the key takeaway is simple.

Microsoft Foundry is not necessarily the next step after Microsoft 365 Copilot or Copilot Studio. It is a different category of capability. It becomes relevant when organizations need to move beyond productivity enhancement and conversational experiences to create AI solutions designed around their own unique business requirements.

Figure 4-8 illustrates how Microsoft Foundry enables organizations to combine AI models, enterprise data, governance controls, and business processes to create tailored AI solutions.

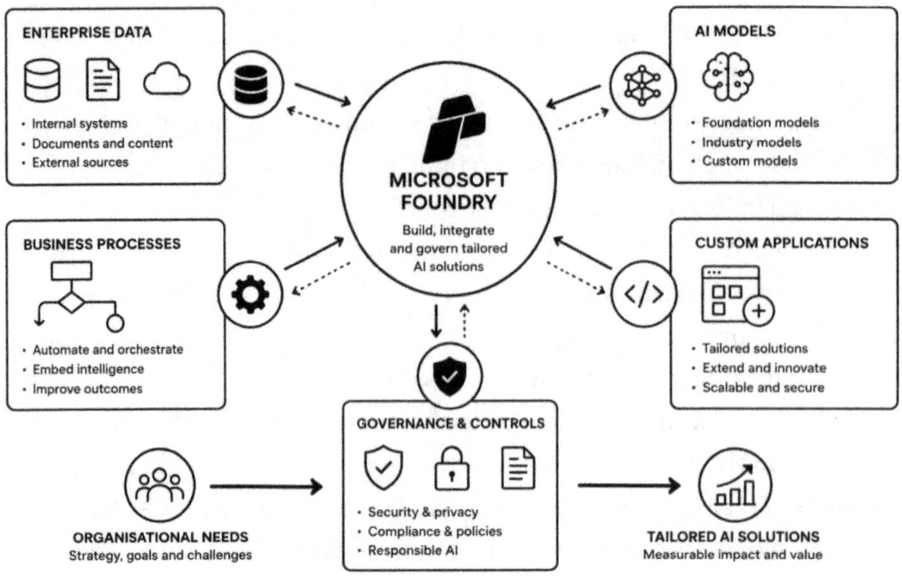

***Figure 4-8.** Building Custom AI Solutions with Microsoft Foundry*

Choosing the Right Microsoft AI Solution

One of the most common questions raised during AI strategy discussions is surprisingly simple:

"Which Microsoft AI solution should we use?"

While the question appears straightforward, the answer is rarely based on technology alone.

Many organizations initially approach AI solution selection by comparing features, capabilities, or product specifications. In practice, successful decisions usually begin somewhere else. They begin with a clear understanding of the business problem.

A useful observation from many AI transformation initiatives is that organizations often struggle more with solution selection than implementation. Once a clear direction has been established, technology teams can usually identify an appropriate architecture, deployment model, and implementation approach. The more difficult challenge is determining which capability is most suitable in the first place.

This is where business context becomes important.

Consider an organization seeking to improve employee productivity. Employees spend significant time reading emails, preparing reports, attending meetings, and searching for information. The primary objective is helping people work more efficiently within tools they already use every day.

In this situation, Microsoft 365 Copilot is often a strong candidate because the value is closely aligned with employee productivity and existing Microsoft 365 workflows.

Now consider a different scenario.

A service desk receives thousands of routine enquiries each month. Employees repeatedly ask the same questions, customers need assistance navigating processes, and support teams spend considerable time responding to requests that follow predictable patterns.

The requirement is no longer centered on personal productivity. Instead, the organization needs a conversational experience capable of guiding users, retrieving information, and supporting business processes.

This type of requirement naturally points toward Copilot Studio.

The situation changes again when organizations require capabilities that extend beyond predefined productivity or conversational experiences.

A business may need an AI solution that integrates multiple data sources, applies specialized business logic, interacts with enterprise systems, and supports a process unique to the organization. The objective is to create something tailored rather than adopt an existing experience.

These requirements often align more closely with Microsoft Foundry.

Notice what is happening in each example.

The technology choice is being driven by the business objective rather than by the popularity of a particular AI platform.

This may sound obvious, yet many organizations take the opposite approach. They begin with a preferred technology and then attempt to fit business requirements around it. The result is often unnecessary complexity, slower adoption, or solutions that fail to deliver expected value.

A more effective approach is to evaluate AI opportunities through a series of practical questions.

Who are the primary users?

Are employees trying to become more productive, or are customers and stakeholders interacting with an AI-powered experience?

How much customization is required?

Can the requirement be addressed using existing capabilities, or does the organization need a solution designed around unique business processes and data?

What level of governance and control is necessary?

Does the solution operate within familiar productivity environments, or does it form part of a broader operational workflow with specific compliance, security, or integration requirements?

These questions often provide more useful guidance than feature comparisons alone.

Interestingly, many successful organizations do not standardize on a single AI capability. They combine multiple capabilities depending on the business need. Employees may use Microsoft 365 Copilot to improve productivity. Customer-facing teams may use Copilot Studio to create conversational experiences. Specialist business functions may rely on custom AI solutions developed through Microsoft Foundry.

Viewed in this way, the Microsoft AI ecosystem becomes less about choosing one product and more about selecting the right capability for the right problem.

This perspective is particularly important for AI Transformation Leaders. The role is not to become an expert in every Microsoft AI offering. The role is to understand enough about each capability to make informed decisions that align technology investments with business outcomes.

Figure 4-9 illustrates how business objectives, user needs, and customization requirements influence the selection of Microsoft 365 Copilot, Copilot Studio, or Microsoft Foundry.

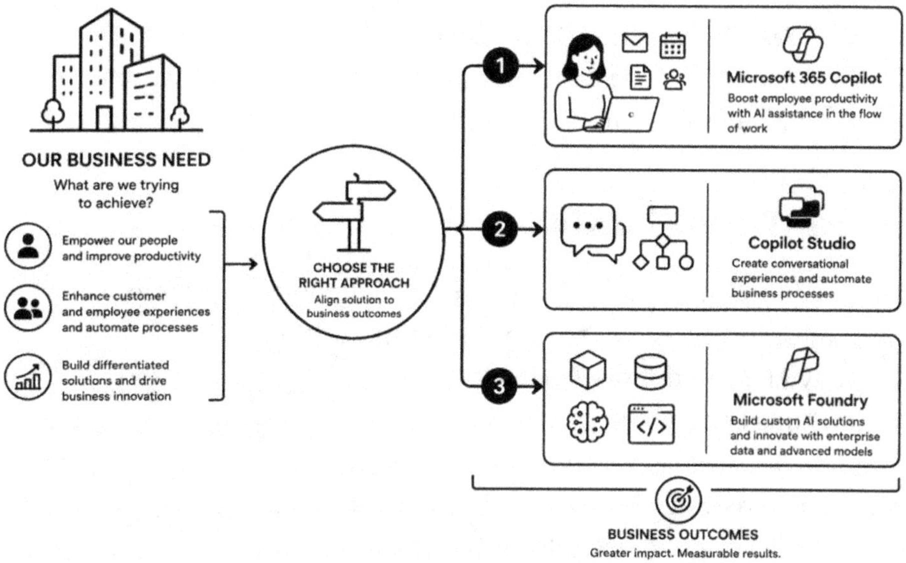

Figure 4-9. *Aligning Business Needs with Microsoft AI Capabilities*

The FIT Framework

By this point, it should be clear that Microsoft 365 Copilot, Copilot Studio, and Microsoft Foundry are designed to address different organizational needs. The challenge for many leaders is not understanding what each capability does, but determining which one is most appropriate for a particular business situation.

During AI strategy discussions, it is easy to become distracted by product features, licensing models, or technical capabilities. While these considerations are important, they often appear later in the decision-making process.

A more effective starting point is understanding the nature of the problem itself.

To support this evaluation, consider the FIT Framework.

FIT is a simple decision model that helps leaders align business needs with the most appropriate Microsoft AI capability.

The framework consists of three perspectives: Familiar Workflows, Interaction and Automation, and Tailored Intelligence.

F—Familiar Workflows

The first question to ask is whether the primary objective is improving how employees work within existing business applications.

Many AI opportunities fall into this category. Employees spend time creating content, reviewing information, preparing presentations, summarizing meetings, responding to emails, and analyzing data. The goal is not to redesign business processes. Instead, it is to help people work more effectively within workflows they already understand.

When the requirement centers on familiar workplace activities, Microsoft 365 Copilot is often the most appropriate starting point.

The emphasis is productivity, adoption, and user enablement rather than custom solution development.

I—Interaction and Automation

The second question is whether the organization needs to create conversational experiences that support employees, customers, partners, or business processes.

In these situations, the focus shifts away from individual productivity and toward interaction.

Users may need guidance, answers, self-service support, or assistance navigating organizational processes. The organization wants to provide a conversational experience that can retrieve information, automate routine activities, and support users at scale.

When interaction and process support become the primary requirement, Copilot Studio is often a natural fit.

The emphasis is creating AI-powered experiences rather than simply improving personal productivity.

T—Tailored Intelligence

The third question is whether the organization requires something uniquely designed around its own data, systems, business processes, or operational requirements.

These situations typically involve greater complexity.

The organization may need specialized integrations, custom workflows, advanced governance controls, industry-specific capabilities, or AI solutions that form part of a broader business process. Existing productivity tools or conversational platforms may not provide sufficient flexibility.

When requirements become highly customized, Microsoft Foundry often becomes the preferred option.

The emphasis is creating tailored AI capabilities rather than adopting predefined experiences.

An important observation is that the FIT Framework is not intended to force every requirement into a single category.

Many organizations operate across all three.

Employees may use Microsoft 365 Copilot for everyday productivity. Customer-facing teams may deploy solutions through Copilot Studio. Specialist business units may invest in custom AI solutions built using Microsoft Foundry.

The value of the framework is not that it produces a perfect answer every time. Its value lies in encouraging leaders to begin with the business objective rather than the technology itself.

When organizations start with the problem, solution selection becomes significantly easier.

Figure 4-10 illustrates how the FIT Framework can be used to align business requirements with Microsoft 365 Copilot, Copilot Studio, and Microsoft Foundry.

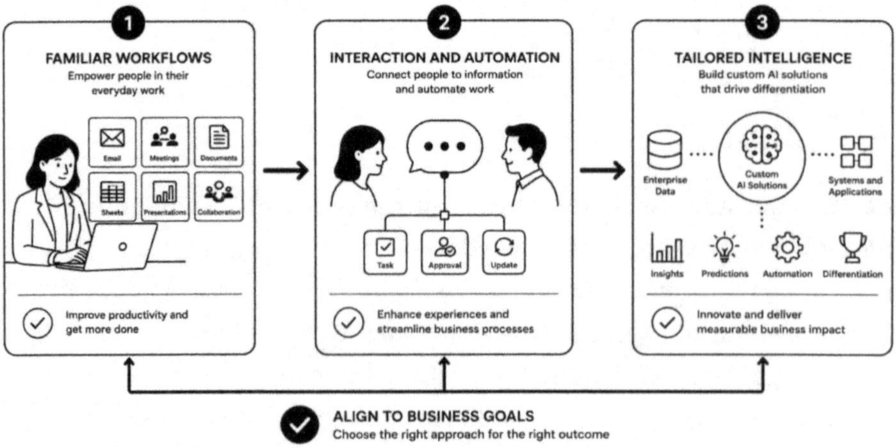

Figure 4-10. *The FIT Framework for Microsoft AI Solution Selection*

Business Scenario Decision-Making

One of the reasons AI solution selection can be challenging is that business requirements rarely arrive neatly categorized.

Leaders are seldom presented with a request that says, "We need Microsoft 365 Copilot," or "We should use Microsoft Foundry." Instead, they are presented with business problems, operational challenges, and opportunities for improvement.

The task is then to determine which capability is most appropriate.

Consider a professional services organization where consultants spend a significant amount of time preparing client presentations, reviewing meeting notes, drafting proposals, and responding to email communication. Leadership wants to improve productivity without fundamentally changing how employees work.

In this situation, the primary challenge is not process automation or custom application development. The organization is seeking efficiency within existing workflows. Using the FIT Framework, this requirement aligns most closely with Familiar Workflows, making Microsoft 365 Copilot a strong candidate.

Now consider a different scenario.

A large organization operates a shared services function that supports employees across multiple business units. Questions about policies, onboarding, expenses, travel procedures, and internal processes consume a considerable amount of support team capacity. Employees often struggle to find information quickly, leading to delays and frustration.

Here, the organization is not simply trying to make individuals more productive. It wants to create a conversational experience that helps users obtain information and complete routine activities independently.

This requirement aligns more closely with Interaction and Automation, making Copilot Studio a logical choice.

The situation changes again when organizations face challenges that are highly specific to their industry or business model.

Imagine an insurance provider that wants to analyze policy documents, claims information, regulatory requirements, and customer interactions to support claims processing. The organization requires specialized workflows, enterprise integrations, governance controls, and business logic tailored to its operations.

Neither a productivity assistant nor a standard conversational solution is likely to address the full requirement.

This is where Tailored Intelligence becomes relevant, pointing toward Microsoft Foundry and the development of a custom AI solution.

What makes these examples interesting is that the technology decision becomes relatively obvious once the business objective is clearly understood.

The difficulty often lies in resisting the temptation to begin with technology.

Many organizations become enthusiastic about a particular AI platform and then attempt to apply it to every scenario. While this approach may appear efficient initially, it frequently results in unnecessary complexity or missed opportunities.

A productivity problem does not always require a custom AI application. Likewise, a highly specialized business process may not be well served by a productivity-focused tool.

The most effective AI Transformation Leaders learn to recognize this distinction early.

They focus on understanding the outcome being sought, the people involved, the complexity of the requirement, and the level of customization required. Only then do they evaluate the available technology options.

Another important observation is that AI adoption rarely follows a single path.

Many organizations begin with Microsoft 365 Copilot because the business case is easy to understand and the value is visible to employees quickly. As adoption matures, they introduce Copilot Studio to improve customer interactions or internal service delivery. Later, they may invest in custom AI solutions through Microsoft Foundry to address strategic business challenges.

This progression is common because organizational confidence in AI often develops gradually.

The goal is not to identify a single platform that solves every problem. The goal is to build an AI portfolio where different capabilities work together to support different business outcomes.

Viewed through this lens, solution selection becomes less about products and more about alignment.

When leaders understand the business objective clearly, the most appropriate Microsoft AI capability often becomes much easier to identify.

Figure 4-11 illustrates how different business scenarios naturally align with Microsoft 365 Copilot, Copilot Studio, and Microsoft Foundry based on the outcomes organizations are trying to achieve.

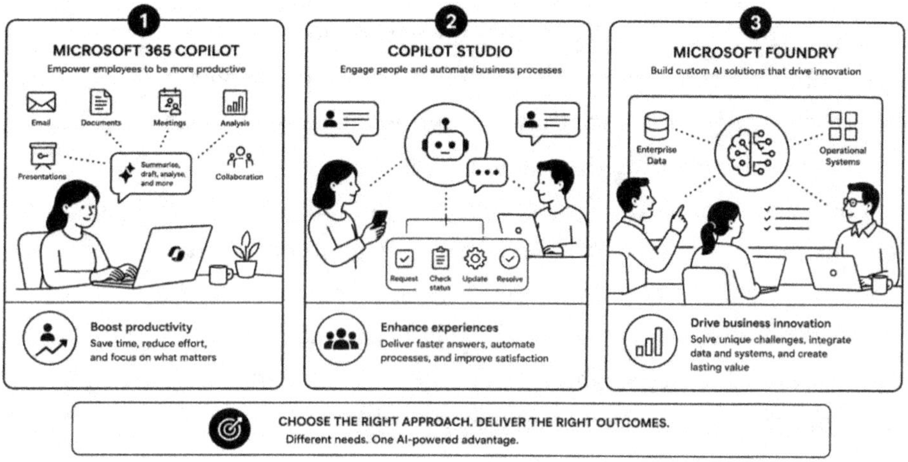

Figure 4-11. *Selecting Microsoft AI Capabilities Based on Business Scenarios*

Leader's Lens

One of the more common patterns in AI transformation programs is that organizations often spend considerable time evaluating technology while spending relatively little time defining the business problem they are trying to solve.

At first glance, this may seem surprising.

Most leadership teams recognize the importance of business value. Yet once AI discussions begin, conversations can quickly shift toward models, platforms, features, integrations, and implementation approaches. Before long, the organization is debating technology choices without first establishing what success actually looks like.

This is where many AI initiatives begin to drift.

The challenge is rarely a lack of technology options. If anything, organizations now have more AI capabilities available than ever before. The real challenge is selecting the capability that best aligns with the outcome being pursued.

One lesson that repeatedly surfaces in transformation programs is that organizations rarely struggle because they lack technology options. More often, they struggle because they are trying to choose a technology before agreeing on the outcome they want to achieve.

The most successful AI programs rarely begin with the most advanced technology. They begin with the clearest business problem.

An organization that understands precisely what it is trying to achieve will usually find it easier to identify an appropriate solution. By contrast, organizations that begin with technology often find themselves searching for problems to justify their investment.

This distinction becomes particularly important when evaluating Microsoft 365 Copilot, Copilot Studio, and Microsoft Foundry.

It is tempting to view these capabilities as stages in a maturity journey, where organizations progress from one to the next as their AI adoption increases. In practice, this is not always the case.

A business may achieve significant value through Microsoft 365 Copilot without ever requiring a custom AI application. Another organization may need Microsoft Foundry from the outset because its primary challenge involves specialized processes, enterprise integrations, or proprietary data. A third organization may find that Copilot Studio delivers the greatest value because improving customer interactions is the immediate priority.

None of these choices is inherently better than the others.

The effectiveness of the decision depends entirely on the business context.

This is one reason experienced AI Transformation Leaders spend less time asking, "Which platform is the most powerful?" and more time asking, "Which capability is most appropriate for the problem we are trying to solve?"

The difference may appear subtle, but it often determines whether an AI initiative creates meaningful business value or becomes an expensive technology experiment.

Another lesson emerges as organizations gain experience with AI adoption.

Successful programs rarely rely on a single capability.

As business needs evolve, different AI solutions often coexist across the organization. Productivity tools support employees. Conversational experiences improve service delivery. Custom AI solutions address specialized business challenges. Together, these capabilities form a broader AI ecosystem that evolves alongside organizational priorities.

The role of leadership is not to choose the most advanced technology available. It is to ensure that technology decisions remain aligned with business outcomes, organizational readiness, and long-term value creation.

When that alignment exists, solution selection becomes significantly easier. When it does not, even the most sophisticated AI platform is unlikely to deliver the results the organization expects.

Exam Trap

In reality, AB-731 rarely rewards technology-first thinking.

The exam consistently favors solutions that align with the business requirement, user needs, and organizational context. This means the correct answer is often the simplest solution capable of achieving the desired outcome rather than the most sophisticated platform available.

Consider a scenario where employees want assistance drafting emails, summarizing meetings, creating presentations, and analyzing information within their everyday work environment.

A common mistake is selecting Microsoft Foundry because it offers the highest level of flexibility and customization.

However, flexibility is not the primary requirement in this situation. The business objective is improving employee productivity within existing Microsoft 365 workflows. Microsoft 365 Copilot is therefore likely to be the more appropriate choice.

Similarly, candidates sometimes assume that every conversational AI requirement should be addressed through custom AI development.

If the organization simply needs a conversational experience that helps employees or customers access information, navigate processes, or complete routine activities, Copilot Studio may provide a more suitable and cost-effective solution than building a fully customized application.

Another common trap involves treating Microsoft 365 Copilot, Copilot Studio, and Microsoft Foundry as competing products.

The Microsoft AI ecosystem is not designed around a single winner.

Many organizations use multiple capabilities simultaneously. Employees may use Microsoft 365 Copilot for productivity, customer-facing teams may deploy solutions through Copilot Studio, and specialized business functions may invest in custom AI solutions built with Microsoft Foundry.

The exam often tests your ability to recognize this distinction.

When evaluating a scenario, avoid asking:

"Which Microsoft AI capability is the most powerful?"

Instead ask:

"What problem is the organization trying to solve?"

If the requirement centers on employee productivity within familiar applications, think Microsoft 365 Copilot.

If the requirement focuses on conversational experiences, self-service interactions, or process guidance, consider Copilot Studio.

If the requirement involves highly customized solutions, specialized integrations, enterprise data, or unique business logic, Microsoft Foundry is often the stronger fit.

The strongest answers usually align technology selection with business outcomes rather than technical capability alone.

This reflects how successful AI adoption decisions are made in practice and is a pattern that appears repeatedly throughout AB-731.

Summary

This chapter explored one of the most important responsibilities facing AI Transformation Leaders: selecting the right AI capability for the right business need.

As AI adoption expands across organizations, the challenge is no longer simply understanding what AI can do. Most leadership teams already recognize the potential of generative AI to improve productivity, enhance customer experiences, and support business innovation. The more difficult task is determining which AI solution is most appropriate for a given scenario.

Throughout the chapter, three key Microsoft AI capabilities were examined: Microsoft 365 Copilot, Copilot Studio, and Microsoft Foundry.

Microsoft 365 Copilot was positioned as a productivity-focused capability designed to help employees work more effectively within familiar Microsoft 365 applications. Its value comes from augmenting everyday activities such as content creation, information retrieval, meeting preparation, communication, and analysis. For many organizations, it represents a practical starting point for AI adoption because employees can experience benefits directly within existing workflows.

The discussion then expanded to Copilot Studio, which addresses a different category of requirement. Rather than improving individual productivity, Copilot Studio enables organizations to create conversational experiences that support employees, customers, partners, and business processes. The focus shifts from helping people perform their work to creating AI-powered interactions that guide, inform, and automate routine activities.

The chapter also explored Microsoft Foundry and its role in supporting custom AI solutions. Unlike predefined productivity or conversational experiences, Microsoft Foundry provides organizations with the flexibility to build AI capabilities tailored to their own data, processes, integrations, and operational requirements. These solutions often become relevant when business needs extend beyond the capabilities offered by existing productivity and conversational platforms.

A recurring theme throughout the chapter was that these capabilities should not be viewed as competing products.

Viewed collectively, Microsoft 365 Copilot, Copilot Studio, and Microsoft Foundry form a complementary ecosystem that supports different stages and dimensions of enterprise AI adoption. The challenge for leaders is not identifying the most powerful capability. It is identifying the most appropriate capability for the outcome being pursued.

As the next chapter explores AI implementation, adoption, and organizational readiness, this principle becomes even more important. Selecting the right technology is only one part of the journey. Long-term success depends on whether organizations can drive adoption, manage change effectively, and translate AI capabilities into measurable business value.

Exam-Style Questions

Question 1

A consulting firm wants to help employees spend less time summarizing meetings, preparing presentations, and responding to emails. Leadership wants a solution that integrates with tools employees already use every day.

Which Microsoft AI capability is the most appropriate starting point?

A. Microsoft Foundry

B. Copilot Studio

C. Microsoft 365 Copilot

D. A custom AI application

Correct Answer

C

Explanation

The primary objective is improving employee productivity within existing Microsoft 365 workflows. Microsoft 365 Copilot is specifically designed for these types of scenarios.

Question 2

An organization receives thousands of repetitive employee enquiries related to travel policies, leave requests, onboarding procedures, and internal processes. Leadership wants employees to receive answers more quickly without increasing support staff.

Which Microsoft AI capability is most appropriate?

A. Microsoft 365 Copilot

B. Copilot Studio

C. Microsoft Foundry

D. PowerPoint Copilot

Correct Answer

B

Explanation

The requirement focuses on creating a conversational experience that helps users access information and navigate business processes. This aligns closely with Copilot Studio.

Question 3

A healthcare provider wants to build an AI solution that combines patient information, organizational policies, enterprise systems, and specialized business rules to support operational decision-making.

Which Microsoft AI capability is most likely required?

A. Microsoft 365 Copilot

B. Outlook Copilot

C. Copilot Studio

D. Microsoft Foundry

Correct Answer

D

Explanation

The organization requires a highly tailored solution involving enterprise data, integrations, governance, and specialized logic. These scenarios typically align with Microsoft Foundry.

Question 4

A leadership team believes Microsoft Foundry should be used for every AI initiative because it provides the highest level of flexibility.

What is the most appropriate response?

A. Flexibility should always take priority over business requirements

B. Every AI requirement should be implemented using custom development

C. The most appropriate solution depends on the business problem being solved

D. Microsoft 365 Copilot should never be used in enterprise environments

Correct Answer

C

Explanation

AB-731 consistently favors business-first decision-making. The most flexible solution is not always the most appropriate solution.

Question 5

An organization has already deployed Microsoft 365 Copilot successfully. Leadership is now exploring ways to improve customer self-service experiences.

What should leaders recognize before selecting a solution?

A. Microsoft 365 Copilot automatically solves all customer interaction scenarios

B. Different business challenges may require different AI capabilities

C. Productivity solutions should always replace conversational experiences

D. Custom AI development is mandatory after deploying Microsoft 365 Copilot

Correct Answer

B

Explanation

Microsoft 365 Copilot, Copilot Studio, and Microsoft Foundry address different business needs and are often used together within the same organization.

Question 6

A retail organization wants customers to ask questions about orders, returns, and store policies through a conversational interface available around the clock.

Which capability is the best fit?

A. Microsoft 365 Copilot

B. Microsoft Foundry

C. Copilot Studio

D. Excel Copilot

Correct Answer

C

Explanation

The organization requires a customer-facing conversational experience rather than employee productivity assistance or a highly customized AI platform.

Question 7

A business wants to improve employee productivity quickly while minimizing implementation complexity and organizational disruption.

Which factor should carry the greatest weight during solution selection?

A. The most advanced AI model available

B. The solution that creates the greatest amount of customization

C. Alignment with existing employee workflows and business objectives

D. The platform requiring the largest implementation effort

Correct Answer

C

Explanation

Successful AI adoption usually begins with business objectives and user needs rather than technical complexity.

Question 8

A leadership team is evaluating a proposed AI initiative. The solution will require access to multiple enterprise systems, specialized business rules, and proprietary organizational data.

Which FIT Framework category best describes this requirement?

A. Familiar Workflows

B. Interaction and Automation

C. Tailored Intelligence

D. Personal Productivity

Correct Answer

C

Explanation

Tailored Intelligence refers to AI solutions designed around unique organizational requirements, data, integrations, and business processes.

Question 9

An organization asks whether Microsoft 365 Copilot, Copilot Studio, and Microsoft Foundry should be viewed as competing products.

Which response best reflects the perspective presented in this chapter?

A. Organizations should choose one platform and avoid the others

B. Microsoft Foundry eventually replaces all other AI capabilities

C. These capabilities address different needs and often complement one another

D. Copilot Studio should always be implemented before Microsoft 365 Copilot

Correct Answer

C

Explanation

The Microsoft AI ecosystem is complementary. Different capabilities support different business objectives and can coexist successfully within the same organization.

Question 10

A manufacturing organization wants to reduce the time engineers spend searching through technical documentation and preparing project updates. The CIO initially proposes building a custom AI application using Microsoft Foundry.

As an AI Transformation Leader, what should you recommend first?

A. Proceed with Microsoft Foundry because custom solutions provide maximum flexibility

B. Evaluate whether Microsoft 365 Copilot can meet the requirement before pursuing custom development

C. Build a conversational assistant using Copilot Studio

D. Delay the initiative until a larger AI strategy is defined

Correct Answer

B

Explanation

The requirement is primarily focused on employee productivity within existing workflows. Leaders should first evaluate whether an existing capability can meet the need before introducing the complexity of custom AI development.

CHAPTER 5

Data, Prompts, and Enterprise Readiness

Introduction

By the time organizations begin evaluating AI capabilities, a common assumption often emerges: if the technology is powerful enough, meaningful results will naturally follow.

Experience suggests otherwise.

Many organizations adopt the same AI tools, access similar models, and invest comparable amounts of effort, yet the outcomes can vary significantly. Some quickly identify measurable business value, while others struggle to move beyond isolated experiments. The difference is rarely explained by the technology alone.

More often, the determining factors are the quality of information available to the organization, the accessibility of that information, the controls surrounding its use, and the clarity with which users communicate their requirements to AI systems.

This is why enterprise AI readiness extends beyond selecting the right platform or deploying the latest capability. Before AI can deliver meaningful outcomes, organizations must ensure that the underlying

K. Shaikh, *Microsoft Certified: AI Transformation Leader Study Companion*, Certification Study Companion Series, https://doi.org/10.1007/979-8-8688-3168-3_5

foundations are in place. Information must be trustworthy. Access must be appropriately governed. Employees must understand how to interact with AI effectively. Without these foundations, even the most advanced AI solution may struggle to produce reliable results.

For leaders, this represents an important shift in thinking.

The conversation is no longer limited to questions such as which AI capability to adopt or which use case to prioritize. Attention must also be given to the information that will support those capabilities and the organizational conditions required for success.

This chapter explores the role of data readiness, enterprise knowledge, security considerations, grounding, and prompting from a leadership perspective. The objective is not to develop technical expertise but to help leaders recognize the factors that influence AI effectiveness within real organizational environments.

Before examining these topics individually, it is useful to understand a simple but often overlooked reality: AI can only create value from the information and direction it receives. Figure 5-1 illustrates how technology, data, context, and user guidance work together to influence AI outcomes.

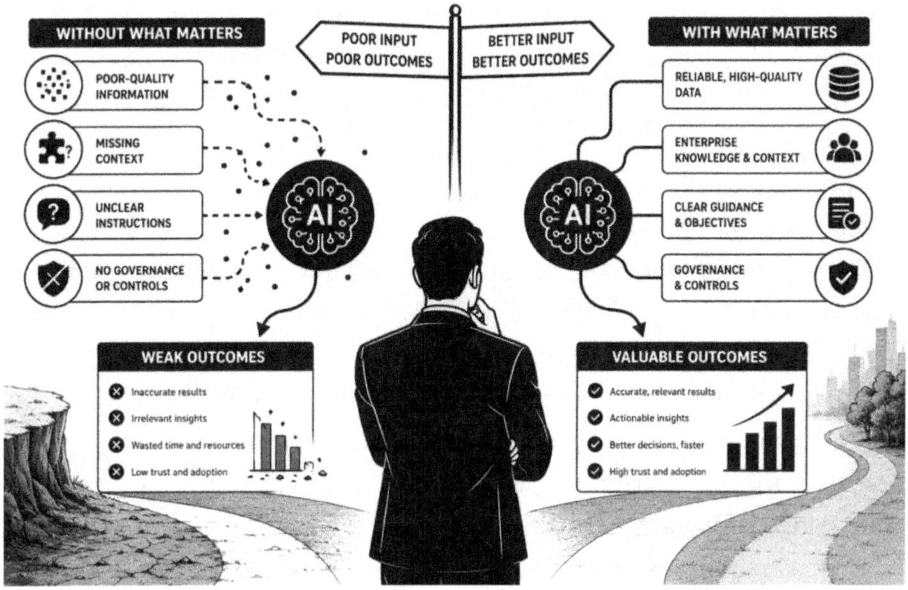

Figure 5-1. *AI Success Depends on More Than the Model*

Why AI Is Only as Good as the Information It Receives

One of the more persistent misconceptions surrounding artificial intelligence is the belief that better technology automatically produces better results.

This assumption is understandable.

The rapid evolution of generative AI has introduced increasingly capable models that can analyze information, generate content, answer questions, and support decision-making in ways that would have seemed remarkable only a few years ago. As a result, organizations often focus their attention on selecting the latest model, the newest AI capability, or the most advanced platform available.

Yet technology alone rarely determines success.

Consider two organizations deploying the same AI capability. Both use similar models, similar infrastructure, and comparable implementation approaches. One organization quickly begins generating value, while the other struggles with inconsistent outputs, low user confidence, and disappointing results.

The difference is often not the AI itself.

The difference is the information available to the AI and the quality of the context surrounding that information.

An AI system can only work with the information it receives. If the information is incomplete, outdated, inaccurate, or difficult to access, the quality of the output will inevitably suffer. Likewise, if users provide limited context or unclear instructions, the resulting responses may fail to meet expectations regardless of how capable the underlying model may be.

This principle is not unique to AI.

Most business decisions are influenced by the quality of information available at the time. Leaders recognize that decisions based on incomplete or unreliable information often carry greater risk. AI systems operate in a similar way. Better information generally enables better outputs, while poor information increases the likelihood of confusion, inconsistency, and error.

This becomes particularly important within enterprise environments.

Many organizations possess large volumes of information accumulated over years of operation. Policies, procedures, customer records, contracts, project documentation, product information, and internal knowledge repositories often contain valuable business knowledge. However, the existence of information does not automatically mean it is ready to support AI.

In some organizations, information may be duplicated across multiple systems. In others, documents may be outdated, difficult to locate, or maintained inconsistently. Employees often compensate for these challenges through experience and organizational knowledge. AI systems, however, depend on the information that is made available to them.

This explains why two organizations using the same technology can experience very different outcomes.

One organization may provide AI with trusted information, clear governance, and relevant business context. Another may provide fragmented knowledge, inconsistent records, and unclear guidance. The technology remains the same, but the quality of the outcomes differs significantly.

For leaders, this creates an important insight.

When AI initiatives fail to deliver expected value, the underlying cause is not always the model, the platform, or the technology provider. In many cases, the real issue lies within the information ecosystem that supports the AI solution.

Organizations that recognize this early often achieve better results because they invest time understanding their information assets before expecting AI to generate business value from them.

This is why enterprise readiness begins with more than technology readiness. Before organizations evaluate prompting techniques, grounding strategies, or advanced AI capabilities, they must first understand the quality, accessibility, and reliability of the information available to the business.

Figure 5-2 illustrates how the same AI capability can produce dramatically different outcomes depending on the quality of information, context, and organizational knowledge it receives.

Figure 5-2. *Same AI, Different Outcomes*

Importance of Data Readiness and Quality

Once leaders recognize that AI outcomes depend heavily on the information available to the organization, a natural question follows.

What makes information ready for AI?

At first glance, the answer may appear straightforward. Most organizations already possess large volumes of data. Customer records, financial systems, operational platforms, knowledge repositories, reports, documents, and communications often contain years of accumulated business information. The challenge is rarely the absence of data.

The challenge is whether that information can be trusted.

Many AI initiatives encounter difficulties not because organizations lack information but because the information itself contains inconsistencies, duplication, gaps, or outdated content. Employees may already be familiar with these issues and have developed workarounds over time. AI systems, however, have no such advantage. They depend on the quality of the information they receive.

This is where data readiness becomes important.

Data readiness is not simply about having large amounts of information available. It is about ensuring that information is sufficiently reliable to support decision-making, business processes, and AI-assisted outcomes.

Consider a customer service environment where customer records are incomplete or inconsistently maintained. Employees may spend time validating information before responding to enquiries because they understand the limitations of the underlying data. If an AI system relies on the same information, it may produce responses that reflect those inaccuracies.

The issue is not that the AI has failed. The issue is that the information supporting the AI was not reliable in the first place.

A similar challenge can occur when organizations maintain multiple versions of the same information. Policies may exist in several locations. Product information may differ between departments. Operational procedures may have evolved without older documentation being updated. Employees often resolve these conflicts through experience and informal knowledge-sharing. AI systems, however, require a clearer source of truth.

This is why data quality should be viewed as a business concern rather than a technical concern.

When leaders hear discussions about data quality, it is easy to assume the responsibility belongs exclusively to technology teams. In reality, many data quality challenges originate within business processes, operational practices, and organizational behaviors.

If information is not maintained consistently, AI cannot compensate for that weakness.

Several characteristics influence whether information is ready to support AI initiatives.

Accuracy remains fundamental. Information should reflect current business realities rather than outdated assumptions or historical conditions that no longer apply.

Completeness is equally important. Missing information can be just as problematic as incorrect information, particularly when AI is expected to provide recommendations, summaries, or responses based on partial context.

Consistency also matters. Information describing the same business entity, process, or activity should not vary significantly across different systems or repositories.

Finally, timeliness plays an important role. Information that was useful six months ago may no longer reflect current products, policies, procedures, or organizational priorities.

Leaders do not need to become experts in data management to appreciate these principles. What they do need to recognize is that poor information quality often appears as poor AI performance.

This distinction is important because it influences how organizations respond when AI outcomes fail to meet expectations.

A common reaction is to evaluate different models, platforms, or technologies. While there may be occasions where technology changes are justified, many AI challenges are ultimately rooted in information quality rather than AI capability.

Organizations that achieve the greatest value from AI often spend significant time improving the quality and reliability of their information before expecting AI to transform business outcomes.

This preparation may not attract the same attention as deploying a new AI capability, but it frequently has a greater impact on long-term success.

For AI Transformation Leaders, the lesson is simple.

Before asking whether the organization is ready for AI, it is worth asking whether the organization's information is ready for AI.

Figure 5-3 illustrates how different dimensions of data quality influence the reliability and usefulness of AI-generated outcomes.

Figure 5-3. *How Data Quality Influences AI Outcomes*

Understanding Enterprise Data

As organizations begin preparing for AI adoption, discussions about data often become increasingly complex. Terms such as structured data, unstructured data, repositories, records, documents, and knowledge sources appear frequently in conversations between business leaders, technology teams, and data specialists.

While leaders are not expected to become data experts, understanding the broad categories of enterprise information can help explain why some AI initiatives are easier to implement than others.

At a high level, organizational information generally falls into two categories: structured data and unstructured data.

Structured data is information organized in a predictable format.

Most business systems rely heavily on structured data. Customer records within a CRM platform, financial transactions within an accounting system, inventory details within a supply chain solution, or employee records within a human resources platform are all common examples.

Because this information follows defined formats and consistent rules, it is generally easier to search, analyze, report on, and manage.

For many years, organizations have used structured data to support reporting, dashboards, analytics, forecasting, and operational decision-making.

However, structured data represents only part of the organizational knowledge landscape.

A significant amount of enterprise knowledge exists in unstructured information.

Unlike structured data, unstructured information does not always follow predefined formats or rigid structures. It often exists within documents, presentations, emails, meeting notes, contracts, policies, procedures, reports, knowledge articles, and other forms of business content.

Consider where employees typically look when they need answers to organizational questions.

They may review policy documents, search knowledge repositories, examine project documentation, read operational guidance, or locate information contained within reports and presentations. Much of this knowledge exists outside traditional databases.

In many organizations, this unstructured information contains some of the most valuable business knowledge available.

It often captures organizational experience, operational procedures, customer insights, product knowledge, lessons learned, and institutional memory accumulated over many years.

Historically, extracting value from this information has been challenging.

Unlike structured records stored in business systems, unstructured content can be difficult to search, organize, and analyze consistently. Employees frequently spend significant amounts of time locating information scattered across multiple locations and formats.

This is one reason generative AI has attracted so much attention.

While earlier generations of technology often focused heavily on structured information, modern AI capabilities are increasingly effective at helping organizations work with large volumes of unstructured content. Documents, reports, policies, meeting notes, and knowledge repositories can now become more accessible through conversational interactions and AI-assisted information retrieval.

For leaders, the key takeaway is not that one type of information is more important than the other.

Both play important roles.

Structured data often provides precision, consistency, and operational accuracy. Unstructured information frequently provides context, organizational knowledge, and business understanding.

The greatest value often emerges when organizations can make both types of information available in ways that support decision-making and business outcomes.

This distinction also helps explain why enterprise readiness extends beyond data quality alone.

An organization may have highly accurate structured data while still struggling to make important organizational knowledge accessible. Equally, an organization may possess extensive documentation but lack the consistency required to support reliable decision-making.

Successful AI initiatives often depend on understanding both dimensions.

Leaders who recognize where organizational knowledge resides are generally better positioned to identify opportunities, anticipate challenges, and make informed decisions about AI adoption.

As organizations seek to improve access to enterprise knowledge, another important consideration emerges. Not all information should be available to everyone. Access permissions, security controls, regulatory obligations, and compliance requirements continue to apply even when AI becomes part of the user experience.

This makes security and governance just as important as data quality when assessing enterprise readiness for AI.

Figure 5-4 illustrates how structured and unstructured information contribute different forms of value within the enterprise knowledge landscape.

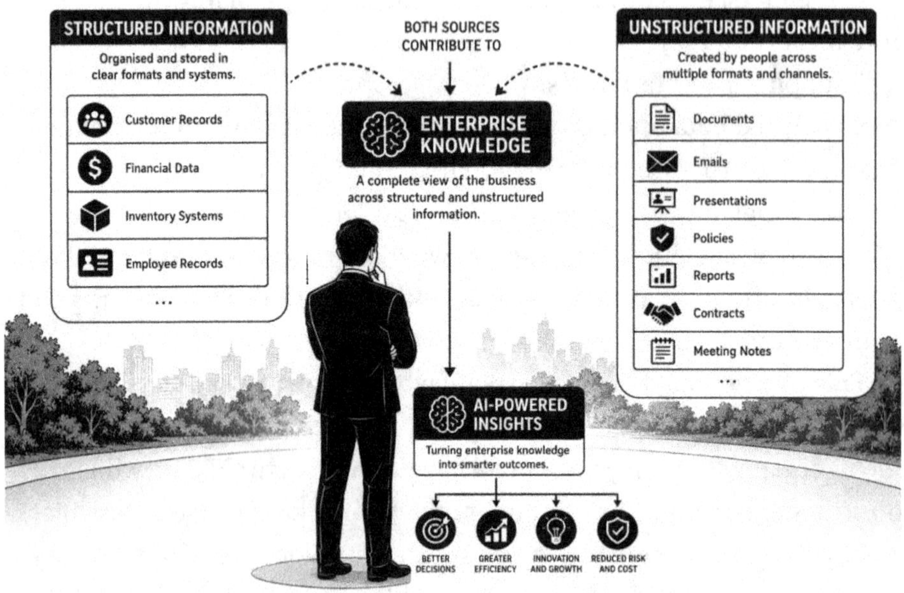

***Figure 5-4.** Where Enterprise Knowledge Lives*

Security, Access, and Compliance Considerations

As organizations explore the potential of AI, enthusiasm often centers on what information can be made available to employees, customers, and business teams. The assumption is straightforward: more information should lead to better outcomes.

While there is some truth in this idea, it only tells part of the story.

Access to information has always required balance. Organizations must ensure that people can obtain the information necessary to perform their roles while simultaneously protecting sensitive, confidential, and regulated information from inappropriate use. The introduction of AI does not remove this responsibility. If anything, it makes it more important.

One of the reasons AI generates excitement is its ability to make information easier to discover and use. Employees no longer need to remember where documents are stored or which department owns a particular process. Instead, they can ask questions using natural language and receive answers quickly.

However, this convenience introduces an important leadership consideration.

AI should make information easier to access, but it should never make information easier to misuse.

This distinction is critical because organizations often manage information with different levels of sensitivity. Financial records, employee information, customer details, legal documents, intellectual property, commercial agreements, and operational procedures may all exist within the same organization, yet not everyone should have access to them.

The same principle applies when AI becomes part of the user experience.

If an employee is not authorized to view certain information through traditional systems, they should not be able to access that information simply by asking an AI assistant. Similarly, customers interacting with AI-powered services should only receive information that is appropriate for their role, permissions, and circumstances.

For leaders, this highlights an important reality.

Successful AI adoption is not only about providing access to knowledge. It is equally about ensuring that existing governance, security controls, and compliance obligations remain intact.

This becomes particularly relevant in highly regulated industries.

Financial institutions must protect customer information. Healthcare providers must safeguard patient records. Government organizations often manage sensitive citizen data. Legal, regulatory, and contractual obligations continue to apply regardless of whether information is accessed through a traditional application, a report, a document repository, or an AI-powered experience.

In many respects, AI should be viewed as another consumer of enterprise information rather than an exception to existing governance practices.

The controls that organizations apply to information today should continue to apply when AI systems retrieve, analyze, summarize, or present that information.

Another challenge emerges when organizations begin connecting AI capabilities to large volumes of enterprise knowledge.

Questions naturally arise.

Who should have access to which information?

How will permissions be respected?

How will sensitive information be protected?

How will organizations ensure compliance with internal policies and external regulations?

These questions are not technical implementation details alone. They are business governance questions that require leadership attention.

One lesson that repeatedly emerges from AI transformation programs is that trust can be lost far more quickly than it can be gained.

Employees are unlikely to trust AI systems that expose inappropriate information. Customers are unlikely to embrace AI-powered services if they believe their information is not being handled responsibly. Regulators are unlikely to overlook governance failures simply because a new technology is involved.

This is why security and compliance should be viewed as foundational elements of enterprise readiness rather than obstacles to innovation.

The most successful organizations recognize that responsible access creates confidence. Confidence encourages adoption. Adoption ultimately determines whether AI delivers meaningful business value.

For AI Transformation Leaders, the objective is not to maximize access at all costs. The objective is to ensure that the right people have access to the right information at the right time while maintaining the controls necessary to protect the organization, its customers, and its stakeholders.

When this balance is achieved, AI can enhance productivity and decision-making without compromising trust.

Figure 5-5 illustrates how organizations can balance information accessibility, governance, and protection when preparing enterprise data for AI-powered experiences.

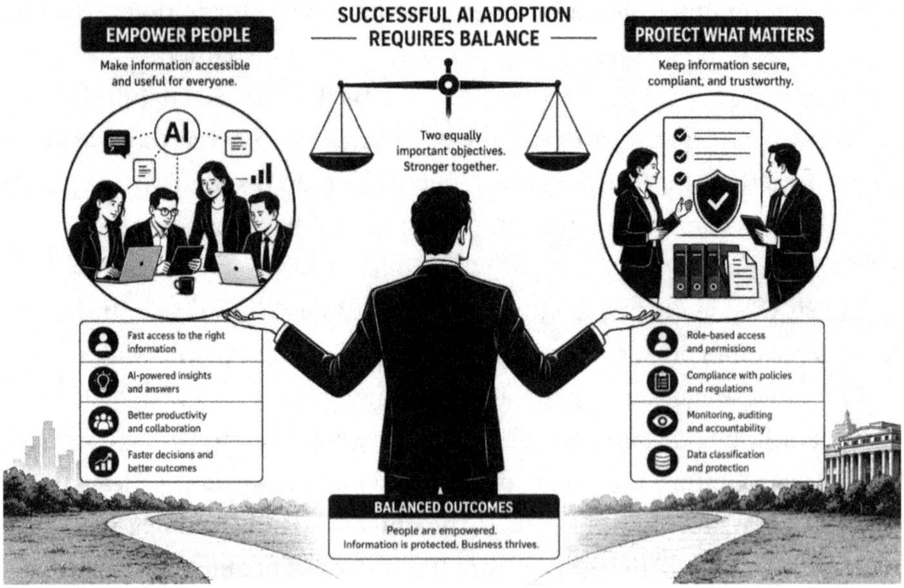

***Figure 5-5.** Balancing Access and Protection*

Grounding AI with Enterprise Data

One of the most common misunderstandings about generative AI is the belief that once an organization adopts an AI capability, the system automatically understands the organization's business, processes, policies, and operational context.

In reality, this is rarely the case.

Modern AI models possess extensive general knowledge acquired during training. They can explain concepts, answer broad questions, generate content, and assist with many common tasks. However, they do not automatically possess detailed knowledge of an individual organization's policies, procedures, products, customers, or internal operations.

This distinction is important because many business questions depend on information that exists only within the organization itself.

An employee may want to understand an internal travel policy. A customer service representative may need information about a specific product offering. A project team may need guidance based on organizational procedures or historical project documentation.

The answers to these questions are often not found within the model itself.

They exist within the organization's information assets.

This is where grounding becomes important.

Grounding refers to the process of providing AI with access to relevant organizational information so that responses can be informed by enterprise knowledge rather than relying solely on general knowledge.

From a leadership perspective, grounding can be viewed as providing context.

Consider a newly hired employee joining an organization.

Even if that individual possesses strong professional skills and broad industry knowledge, they still require access to organizational information before they can make informed decisions. They need to understand policies, procedures, products, customers, terminology, and operational practices.

AI operates in a similar way.

General knowledge provides a useful foundation, but organizational context is often required to generate responses that are accurate, relevant, and aligned with business needs.

This explains why grounding has become such an important topic within enterprise AI discussions.

Without organizational context, AI may generate responses that are technically plausible but not necessarily relevant to the organization using it. The information may be accurate in a general sense while still failing to address the specific business question being asked.

With appropriate organizational context, however, responses can become significantly more useful.

Employees can receive guidance based on current policies. Customer-facing teams can access relevant product information. Business users can retrieve knowledge from trusted organizational sources rather than relying solely on personal experience or manual searches.

The value is not simply improved accuracy.

Grounding can also improve consistency.

In many organizations, different employees may answer the same question in different ways depending on their experience, interpretation, or familiarity with available information. When AI is able to reference trusted organizational knowledge, responses become more aligned with approved information and established business practices.

This can be particularly valuable within large organizations where knowledge is distributed across departments, locations, systems, and repositories.

Another benefit is efficiency.

Employees often spend considerable time searching for information that already exists somewhere within the organization. Policies, procedures, reports, project documents, and knowledge articles may all be available, yet locating the right information at the right moment can still be difficult.

Grounded AI experiences can help reduce this effort by connecting users with relevant information more quickly.

However, grounding should not be viewed as a substitute for information quality.

If organizational information is outdated, inconsistent, or poorly governed, grounding AI to that information may simply reproduce those weaknesses at scale. This is one reason data readiness, governance, and security remain essential considerations.

Effective grounding depends on trusted information sources.

For leaders, the key lesson is straightforward.

The value of enterprise AI is often determined not only by the capability of the model but also by the quality of the organizational knowledge available to support it.

Many AI initiatives focus heavily on selecting models, platforms, and features. While these decisions are important, the long-term value frequently comes from enabling AI to operate with relevant business context.

When organizations provide AI with reliable information, appropriate permissions, and meaningful context, the technology becomes significantly more capable of supporting business outcomes.

Figure 5-6 illustrates the difference between AI operating with general knowledge alone and AI operating with access to trusted organizational context.

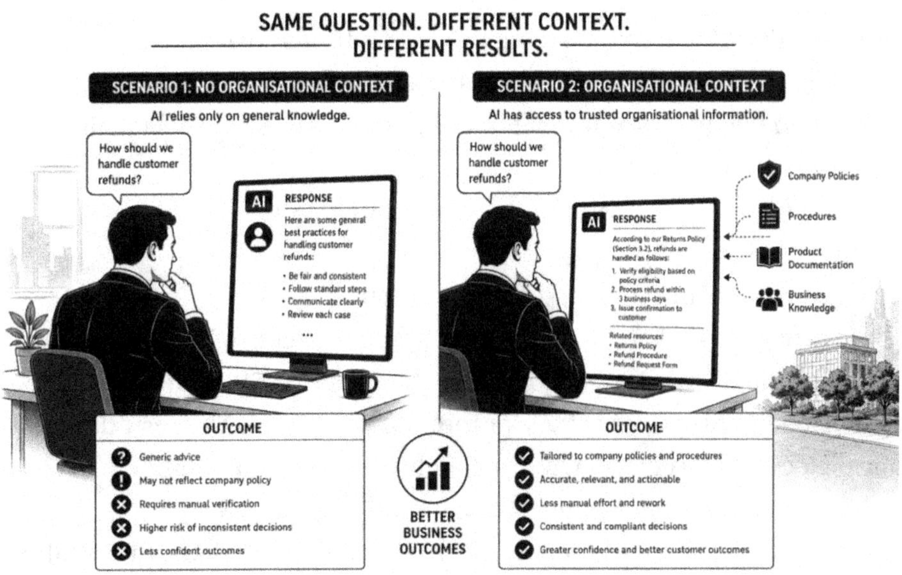

Figure 5-6. *From General Knowledge to Organizational Context*

Prompt Engineering Concepts for Leaders

As organizations become more familiar with generative AI, an interesting pattern often emerges.

Two employees can use the same AI capability, ask what appears to be a similar question, and receive very different results. One employee may find the response useful and relevant, while the other concludes that the technology failed to meet expectations.

In many cases, the difference is not the AI itself.

The difference is how the request was communicated.

This observation introduces one of the most important concepts in generative AI: prompting.

At its simplest level, a prompt is the instruction, question, or request provided to an AI system. It represents the starting point for the interaction and helps the AI understand what the user is trying to achieve.

While prompting is often discussed as a technical skill, leaders do not need to become prompt engineering specialists to appreciate its importance.

In many respects, prompting is less about technology and more about communication.

Consider a common workplace situation.

A manager asks a team member to prepare a report. If the request contains little detail, the employee may be uncertain about the audience, level of detail, format, priorities, or intended outcome. The resulting report may be technically correct while still failing to meet expectations.

The same principle applies when interacting with AI.

When instructions are vague, incomplete, or ambiguous, the resulting output may lack relevance or clarity. Conversely, when expectations are communicated clearly, the AI is generally better positioned to produce a useful response.

This is one reason organizations often discover that effective AI use requires new habits rather than entirely new technologies.

Users who provide context, explain objectives, identify constraints, and clarify expectations frequently achieve better results than those who simply ask broad or generic questions.

For leaders, several concepts are particularly useful to understand.

The first is context.

AI performs more effectively when it understands the situation surrounding the request. Information about the audience, business objective, organizational environment, or intended outcome can help improve the relevance of the response.

The second is clarity.

Requests that clearly describe the desired outcome often produce more useful results than requests that leave significant room for interpretation. Clear communication reduces ambiguity for both people and AI systems.

The third is constraints.

In business environments, responses are rarely generated without boundaries. A user may need information presented in a specific format, tailored for a particular audience, or aligned with defined organizational requirements. Communicating these expectations helps guide the AI toward a more appropriate result.

Finally, there is iteration.

Many users initially assume that AI interactions should produce perfect results from a single request. In practice, effective use often involves refinement. Additional context, clarification, and follow-up questions can progressively improve the quality of the output.

This should not be viewed as a limitation.

Most professional work involves iteration. Presentations are revised. Reports are reviewed. Strategies are refined. AI interactions often follow a similar pattern.

An important leadership lesson emerges from these observations.

Many issues attributed to AI performance are actually communication issues.

Users may conclude that the technology lacks capability when the underlying challenge is that the request did not provide sufficient context or direction. Organizations that recognize this distinction are often more successful in helping employees adopt AI effectively.

This is also why training programs focused solely on technology features rarely deliver the desired outcomes. Employees benefit not only from understanding what AI can do but also from understanding how to communicate objectives, expectations, and requirements clearly.

The goal is not to teach everyone advanced prompting techniques.

The goal is to help people communicate with AI in ways that support better business outcomes.

For AI Transformation Leaders, the key takeaway is simple.

Prompting should be viewed as a business skill as much as a technology skill. The ability to provide context, define objectives, communicate constraints, and refine requests can have a significant influence on the value employees obtain from AI systems.

When combined with trusted data, appropriate governance, and organizational context, effective prompting becomes another important contributor to successful AI adoption.

Figure 5-7 illustrates how context, clarity, constraints, and iteration influence the quality of AI-generated responses.

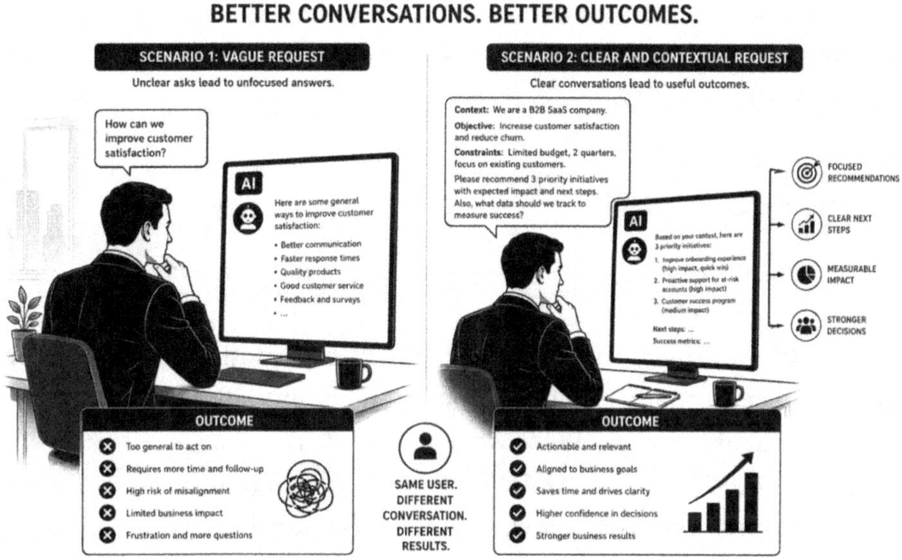

***Figure 5-7.** How Better Instructions Produce Better Outcomes*

The READY Framework

Throughout this chapter, a recurring theme has emerged.

The success of enterprise AI is influenced by far more than the capability of the model itself.

Organizations often focus significant attention on selecting platforms, evaluating features, and identifying use cases. While these decisions are important, they represent only part of the readiness equation. Long-term success depends on whether AI has access to trusted information, meaningful context, appropriate governance, and clear user guidance.

For leaders, assessing these factors can sometimes feel overwhelming.

To simplify this evaluation, consider the READY Framework.

READY provides a practical way to assess whether an organization has established the foundations necessary for successful AI adoption.

The framework consists of five elements: Reliable Data, Enterprise Context, Access Control, Direction Through Prompts, and Yield Business Value.

R—Reliable Data

The first question leaders should ask is whether the organization's information can be trusted.

AI systems depend on the quality of the information available to them. If data is inaccurate, incomplete, inconsistent, or outdated, the resulting outputs are likely to reflect those weaknesses.

Reliable data does not require perfection. Few organizations possess flawless information assets. However, leaders should have confidence that the information supporting AI initiatives is sufficiently accurate and trustworthy to support business decisions and operational activities.

When organizations struggle with information quality, AI often exposes those weaknesses rather than solving them.

E—Enterprise Context

The second consideration is whether AI has access to the organizational knowledge required to support meaningful outcomes.

General knowledge can be useful, but many business questions depend on information that exists only within the organization itself. Policies, procedures, product documentation, operational guidance, and institutional knowledge often provide the context necessary for relevant and accurate responses.

Leaders should therefore consider whether important organizational knowledge is accessible, current, and available to support AI-powered experiences.

The more effectively AI can understand organizational context, the more useful it becomes to employees and business users.

A—Access Control

The third element focuses on governance, security, and responsible access.

AI should respect the same permissions, policies, and compliance requirements that apply throughout the organization. Employees should only access information appropriate to their roles, and sensitive information should remain protected regardless of how it is accessed.

Access control is not simply a technical safeguard. It is a foundation for trust.

When employees, customers, and stakeholders believe information is being handled responsibly, confidence in AI adoption increases significantly.

D—Direction Through Prompts

The fourth element recognizes that AI effectiveness depends not only on information but also on communication.

Even when reliable information and organizational context are available, users must still provide sufficient direction to help AI understand what is required.

Clear objectives, relevant context, defined constraints, and iterative refinement often contribute significantly to the quality of AI-generated outputs.

This is why organizations should view prompting as a practical business skill rather than a specialist technical capability.

Y—Yield Business Value

The final question is perhaps the most important.

Will the AI initiative create meaningful business value?

Organizations sometimes become focused on technology capabilities while losing sight of the outcomes they are trying to achieve. Improved productivity, better customer experiences, faster decision-making, reduced operational effort, and increased organizational effectiveness are all examples of outcomes that may justify investment in AI.

Ultimately, readiness should not be measured solely by technical capability.

It should be measured by the organization's ability to translate AI capabilities into tangible business results.

Taken together, the READY Framework provides leaders with a simple but effective way to evaluate organizational preparedness for AI.

It does not replace detailed planning, governance, or implementation activities. Rather, it serves as a practical reminder that successful AI adoption depends on a combination of trusted information, organizational knowledge, responsible access, effective communication, and measurable outcomes.

When these elements are present, organizations are generally far better positioned to realize the value that AI can offer.

Figure 5-8 illustrates how the five components of the READY Framework work together to support enterprise AI readiness and business value creation.

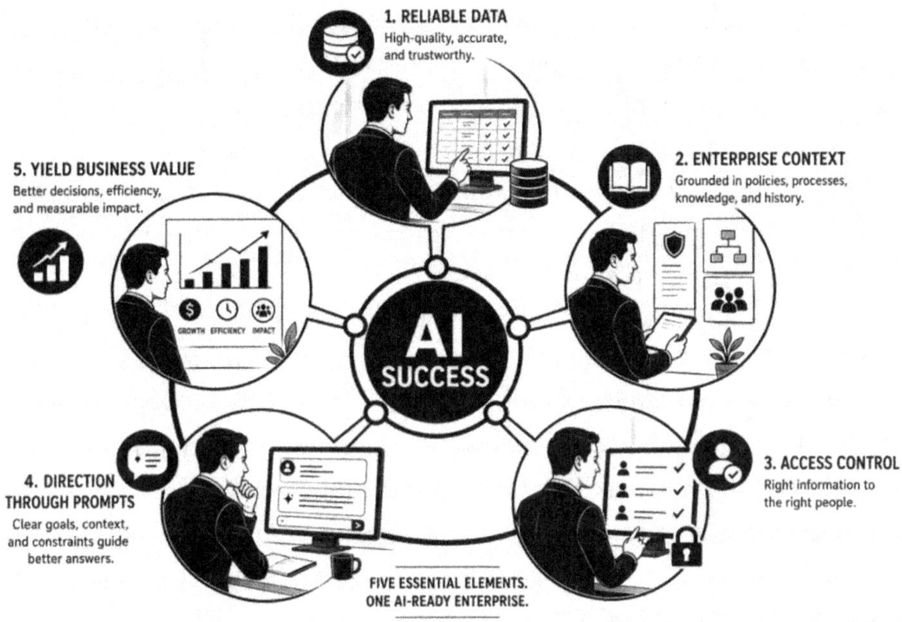

Figure 5-8. *The READY Framework for Enterprise AI Readiness*

Leader's Lens

One lesson tends to surface repeatedly across AI transformation programs.

When organizations become disappointed with AI outcomes, the initial reaction is often to question the technology.

Leaders may wonder whether a different model is needed. Teams may explore alternative platforms. Discussions frequently focus on new features, additional capabilities, or the next generation of AI technology.

Occasionally, these actions are justified. More often, however, the underlying issue lies somewhere else.

Many AI problems that appear to be model problems are actually data, context, or readiness problems.

This distinction is important because it influences how organizations respond when expectations are not being met.

Consider a situation where employees report that AI-generated responses are inconsistent. The immediate assumption may be that the technology lacks capability. Yet a closer examination often reveals that different users are accessing different sources of information, relying on outdated content, or providing insufficient context within their requests.

The technology is functioning as expected; the challenge exists within the environment supporting it.

A similar pattern appears when organizations struggle to realize value from AI investments. Leadership teams may conclude that adoption is lower than expected because employees do not recognize the potential benefits. In reality, employees may be encountering information that is difficult to trust, responses that lack organizational context, or outputs that require significant manual correction before they can be used confidently.

Again, the issue is not necessarily the model; it is the readiness of the organization to support effective AI usage.

Over time, many successful organizations come to recognize a simple but important principle.

AI amplifies the strengths and weaknesses that already exist within the business.

Well-managed information becomes more valuable when AI helps people access it efficiently. Clear governance becomes more important when information can be retrieved through conversational interactions. Effective communication becomes more influential when users rely on prompts to guide AI behavior.

The opposite is also true.

Poor information quality becomes more visible. Inconsistent processes become more apparent. Weak governance becomes more difficult to ignore. AI rarely creates these challenges. It often exposes them.

This is one reason readiness deserves leadership attention long before organizations begin measuring productivity gains or evaluating return on investment.

The organizations that derive the greatest value from AI are not always those with the largest technology budgets or the most sophisticated platforms. More often, they are the organizations that understand their information, govern it effectively, make it accessible responsibly, and help employees use AI with confidence.

Technology remains important; however, technology alone rarely determines success.

As AI capabilities continue to evolve, the organizations most likely to benefit will not necessarily be those that adopt every new innovation first. They will be the organizations that build strong foundations and create an environment where AI can operate with trusted information, meaningful context, and clear direction.

For AI Transformation Leaders, this perspective is worth remembering.

When an AI initiative struggles, the first question should not always be, "Do we need a better model?"

Sometimes the more useful question is:

"Have we provided the model with everything it needs to succeed?"

Exam Trap

One of the most common mistakes made during AI initiatives is assuming that better technology automatically produces better outcomes.

At first glance, this assumption appears reasonable. Generative AI capabilities continue to improve rapidly, new models are released regularly, and organizations often hear success stories describing impressive productivity gains and business benefits.

As a result, when AI-generated outputs fail to meet expectations, many leaders instinctively look toward the technology itself for answers.

Questions quickly emerge.

Do we need a more advanced model? Should we upgrade to a different platform? Would another AI capability produce better results?

While these may be valid questions in some situations, they often distract from a more important issue.

AB-731 repeatedly emphasizes that successful AI adoption depends on more than model capability alone.

A powerful AI model cannot compensate for poor-quality information.

It cannot reliably overcome incomplete organizational context.

It cannot eliminate governance weaknesses.

It cannot consistently produce meaningful outcomes when users provide unclear objectives or insufficient guidance.

In other words, technology alone cannot solve readiness problems.

Consider a scenario where employees report inconsistent AI responses. A common reaction is to assume that the AI capability is underperforming. However, the more appropriate response may be to examine the information being used, the sources available to the AI, the permissions governing access, and the quality of the instructions being provided by users.

Similarly, organizations sometimes believe that introducing a more advanced model will automatically improve business outcomes. Yet if underlying information remains inaccurate, fragmented, or outdated, the organization may simply receive faster answers based on poor information.

The technology improves. The underlying problem remains.

This distinction is important because it reflects how AI transformation decisions are made in practice.

When evaluating AI opportunities, leaders should avoid focusing exclusively on the sophistication of the technology. Equal attention should be given to data quality, organizational knowledge, security controls, governance requirements, and user readiness.

The strongest answers in AB-731 are rarely those that select the most powerful technology option available.

Instead, they are the answers that recognize the relationship between technology capability and organizational readiness.

Before choosing a new model, ask whether the organization has trusted information.

Before introducing additional AI capabilities, ask whether employees have access to the context they need.

Before expecting better outcomes, ask whether users understand how to communicate effectively with AI.

These questions often reveal the true source of the challenge.

For exam purposes, remember this principle:

If an AI initiative is struggling, do not assume the model is the problem first. Evaluate data quality, enterprise context, governance, access controls, and user guidance before concluding that a technology change is required.

Summary

This chapter explored an important reality that is sometimes overlooked during AI transformation initiatives: successful AI outcomes depend on more than the technology itself.

As organizations evaluate AI opportunities, it is easy to focus attention on models, platforms, and capabilities. While these elements remain important, they represent only part of the equation. The value generated by AI is heavily influenced by the information available to the organization, the context provided to the AI, the controls governing access, and the quality of user interactions.

Concepts were brought together through the READY Framework: Reliable Data, Enterprise Context, Access Control, Direction Through Prompts, and Yield Business Value. The framework provides leaders with a practical way to assess whether their organization has established the foundations necessary for successful AI adoption.

Ultimately, enterprise AI readiness is not determined by the sophistication of the model alone. It is determined by the organization's ability to provide trusted information, meaningful context, responsible governance, and clear direction.

Organizations that invest in these foundations are generally better positioned to realize sustainable value from AI technologies and to support adoption with confidence.

As the next chapter explores AI adoption, governance, and scaling strategies, this perspective becomes even more important. Selecting the right AI capability and preparing organizational information are critical foundations, but they represent only the beginning of the transformation journey. Long-term success depends on establishing appropriate governance, encouraging responsible adoption, building organizational trust, and creating the structures necessary to scale AI sustainably across the enterprise. Organizations that combine strong foundations with effective adoption and governance practices are far more likely to realize lasting business value from their AI investments.

Figure 5-9 brings these ideas together, showing how reliable data, enterprise context, appropriate access controls, effective prompting, and a clear focus on business value work together to create an AI-ready enterprise.

Figure 5-9. *Building an AI-Ready Enterprise*

Exam-Style Questions

Question 1

A leadership team is disappointed with the quality of responses being generated by its AI solution. Several stakeholders immediately suggest upgrading to a more advanced AI model.

Before making that decision, what should the organization evaluate first?

A. Whether a larger model is available

B. Whether users have received AI training

C. The quality, accuracy, and accessibility of the information being provided to the AI

D. Whether competitors are using a different AI platform

Correct Answer

C

Explanation

Many AI challenges originate from poor information quality rather than limitations in the model itself. Leaders should assess data readiness before assuming a technology change is required.

Question 2

A leadership team is assessing whether existing information assets can support AI adoption. The organization maintains structured customer records alongside large volumes of reports, policies, emails, and operational documents. What should leaders recognize?

A. Only customer data contributes to AI readiness

B. Organizational knowledge often exists across both structured and unstructured information

C. Unstructured information is not relevant to generative AI

D. AI should only use information stored within databases

Correct Answer

B

Explanation

Enterprise knowledge frequently spans both structured records and unstructured content. Successful AI initiatives often depend on leveraging both.

Question 3

A project team wants employees to receive answers based on current organizational policies and approved procedures rather than relying solely on general AI knowledge.

Which concept is most relevant?

A. Scaling

B. Automation

C. Grounding

D. Forecasting

Correct Answer

C

Explanation

Grounding helps AI provide responses informed by trusted organizational information and enterprise context.

Question 4

An organization is preparing for a major AI rollout. The leadership team wants to ensure employees can access information efficiently while still protecting sensitive data.

Which principle should guide decision-making?

A. AI should provide unrestricted access to all organizational information

B. Productivity should take priority over governance

C. Information accessibility and protection should be balanced

D. Security controls should be reduced to encourage adoption

Correct Answer

C

Explanation

Successful AI adoption requires organizations to balance access, governance, compliance, and protection.

Question 5

Two employees use the same AI capability to prepare a customer communication. One receives a highly relevant response, while the other receives a generic result.

What is the most likely explanation?

A. The AI changed its underlying model

B. The employees were using different operating systems

C. The quality of context and instructions provided to the AI differed

D. The AI performed incorrectly for one user

Correct Answer

C

Explanation

Prompt quality, context, and clarity often influence the usefulness of AI-generated responses.

Question 6

During an AI readiness assessment, leadership discovers that important business information exists across multiple repositories and that different departments maintain conflicting versions of the same content.

What risk does this create?

A. Increased model performance

B. Reduced governance requirements

C. Inconsistent AI-generated outputs

D. Faster user adoption

Correct Answer

C

Explanation

When information sources are inconsistent, AI may generate responses that vary depending on which information is accessed.

Question 7

A senior executive states:

"We have selected a leading AI platform, so readiness should no longer be a concern."

As an AI Transformation Leader, how should you respond?

A. Platform selection automatically guarantees success

B. Readiness remains important because AI outcomes depend on information quality, context, governance, and user guidance

C. Governance becomes less important once AI is deployed

D. User adoption is unrelated to readiness

Correct Answer

B

Explanation

Technology selection is only one component of enterprise AI readiness.

Question 8

A business unit wants AI to assist employees with internal procedures, product information, and operational guidance.

According to the READY Framework, which element is most directly concerned with making organizational knowledge available to AI?

A. Reliable Data

B. Enterprise Context

C. Access Control

D. Yield Business Value

Correct Answer

B

Explanation

Enterprise Context focuses on ensuring AI can utilize relevant organizational knowledge to support meaningful outcomes.

Question 9

An organization invests heavily in AI technology but provides little guidance on how employees should interact with AI systems.

Which READY Framework element is most likely being overlooked?

A. Direction Through Prompts

B. Reliable Data

C. Enterprise Context

D. Access Control

Correct Answer

A

Explanation

Even powerful AI capabilities require clear instructions, context, and guidance to produce effective business outcomes.

Question 10

A leadership team is reviewing several AI initiatives and wants to determine whether the organization is truly prepared for broader adoption.

Which question is most aligned with the READY Framework?

A. Which department has the largest technology budget?

B. Which AI model has the highest number of parameters?

C. Does the organization have trusted information, appropriate governance, organizational context, and effective user guidance?

D. How many AI tools have been deployed during the past year?

Correct Answer

C

Explanation

The READY Framework emphasizes readiness through reliable data, enterprise context, access control, direction through prompts, and business value rather than technology metrics alone.

CHAPTER 6

Adoption, Governance, and Scaling AI

Introduction

Many organizations successfully build AI pilots. Far fewer successfully transform their business. The difference is rarely the technology; it is leadership.

It demonstrates that the technology works, that business users can see its potential, and that leadership has taken an important first step toward AI-driven transformation.

However, a successful pilot should never be mistaken for a successful transformation.

Many organizations launch AI initiatives with enthusiasm, identify promising use cases, and generate positive feedback from early adopters. Yet months later, the anticipated business value has not materialized. Adoption slows, different departments begin experimenting independently, governance becomes inconsistent, and leadership starts questioning whether the investment has delivered the expected return.

These situations are surprisingly common, and they rarely occur because the AI technology itself is inadequate.

K. Shaikh, *Microsoft Certified: AI Transformation Leader Study Companion*, Certification Study Companion Series, https://doi.org/10.1007/979-8-8688-3168-3_6

More often, organizations discover that introducing AI into everyday business operations requires much more than selecting the right platform or deploying the right solution. Employees need confidence in how AI should be used. Leaders need governance mechanisms that encourage innovation while managing risk. Business units need clear ownership, consistent decision-making, and a shared vision for how AI supports organizational objectives.

In other words, the challenge shifts from implementing AI to integrating AI into the way the organization operates. This distinction is an important one.

Implementation is often measured by technical milestones such as deployment, configuration, or availability. Transformation is measured differently. It is reflected in how consistently AI is adopted, how effectively it supports business processes, how responsibly it is governed, and whether it continues to create value as its use expands across the organization.

Throughout this book, we have progressively built the foundations required for this stage of the journey.

Chapter 3 introduced the principles of Responsible AI and demonstrated why trust, transparency, and accountability are essential leadership responsibilities.

Chapter 4 examined Microsoft's AI ecosystem and explored how leaders can select the most appropriate AI capability for different business scenarios.

Chapter 5 focused on enterprise readiness, showing that trusted information, organizational context, security, and effective prompting all influence the quality of AI outcomes.

This chapter brings those ideas together and shifts the conversation toward organizational execution.

Rather than asking, *"Which AI capability should we use?"*, leaders now face a different set of questions:

- How should AI initiatives be governed as they grow?
- Who should make decisions about AI investments and organizational standards?
- How can employees be encouraged to adopt AI confidently and responsibly?
- How should success be measured beyond the completion of a pilot?

And perhaps most importantly, how can organizations scale AI in a way that remains sustainable over time?

These are leadership questions rather than technical questions, and they often determine whether AI becomes a strategic business capability or simply another technology experiment.

As AI continues to evolve, organizations that succeed will not necessarily be those that adopt AI first. They will be the organizations that establish clear governance, enable their workforce, encourage responsible innovation, and create the organizational structures needed to support AI at enterprise scale.

Figure 6-1 illustrates this transition from isolated AI pilots to sustainable enterprise transformation, highlighting how governance, adoption, and responsible scaling work together to turn promising technology into lasting business value.

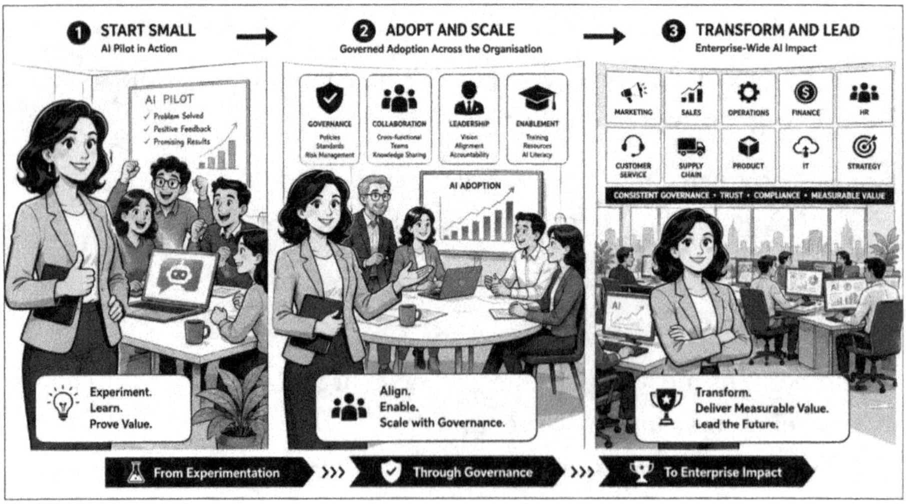

Figure 6-1. *From AI Pilot to Enterprise Transformation*

Establishing Governance Before Scale

One of the most common patterns seen during AI transformation is that governance receives attention only after AI adoption has already begun to accelerate.

The sequence is understandable.

A business unit identifies an opportunity to improve productivity, a successful pilot demonstrates encouraging results, and enthusiasm spreads across the organization. Other departments begin exploring their own AI use cases, employees experiment with new capabilities, and leaders see growing demand for wider adoption.

At first, this appears to be a sign of success.

However, as AI usage expands, organizations often begin encountering new questions that were not apparent during the pilot phase.

Should every department be allowed to procure its own AI tools?

Who decides which use cases should be prioritized?

How should sensitive information be protected when AI becomes part of everyday work?

Who is accountable if an AI-assisted decision leads to an unexpected business outcome?

How should regulatory obligations, organizational policies, and Responsible AI principles be applied consistently across different business functions?

These questions rarely emerge because the technology has failed.

They emerge because the organization has reached a point where informal decision-making is no longer sufficient.

This is where governance becomes essential.

Unfortunately, governance is sometimes misunderstood as a mechanism for slowing innovation. Teams may worry that introducing governance will create unnecessary approvals, increase bureaucracy, or discourage experimentation.

In practice, effective governance achieves the opposite.

Good governance provides clarity.

It helps employees understand which AI solutions are approved, how organizational information should be used, who is responsible for key decisions, and how innovation can take place within clearly defined boundaries. Rather than preventing progress, governance creates the confidence needed for organizations to expand AI adoption responsibly.

This distinction is particularly important for AI Transformation Leaders.

Unlike many traditional technology initiatives, AI often influences decisions, recommendations, and business processes that extend beyond a single department. Marketing may use AI to create content. Human resources may explore AI-assisted recruitment. Finance may evaluate AI-supported forecasting. Customer service teams may rely on AI to improve response times.

Each initiative may deliver value individually; yet without shared governance, organizations can quickly find themselves operating with inconsistent standards, duplicated effort, and varying approaches to risk management.

Governance provides the common foundation that allows innovation to occur consistently across the enterprise.

Importantly, governance should not be viewed solely as the responsibility of technology teams.

Decisions about acceptable AI use, organizational risk, regulatory obligations, ethical considerations, and business priorities require participation from multiple functions. Legal specialists, risk managers, security teams, compliance officers, business leaders, human resources, and technology teams each contribute different perspectives that help organizations make balanced decisions.

This collaborative approach reflects an important principle introduced in Chapter 3.

Responsible AI is not achieved through technology alone. It is achieved through leadership, accountability, and governance that are embedded within organizational decision-making.

Another misconception is that governance must be fully defined before any AI experimentation can begin.

Most organizations do not start with a comprehensive governance framework.

Instead, governance often matures alongside adoption. Initial pilots help leaders understand where guidance is needed, which risks require closer attention, and how responsibilities should evolve as AI becomes more widely used. The important consideration is that governance grows intentionally rather than reactively.

When governance is postponed until AI has already spread across the organization, leaders often face a much more difficult challenge. Different departments may have adopted different tools, established inconsistent practices, or created conflicting policies that are difficult to standardize later.

Building governance before large-scale adoption is usually far easier than trying to introduce consistency after fragmentation has already occurred.

For AI Transformation Leaders, the objective is not to create additional layers of control.

The objective is to create an environment where innovation can expand with confidence because employees understand the principles, responsibilities, and decision-making processes that guide the organization's use of AI.

As governance becomes more structured, another question naturally follows.

Who should own these decisions?

In most successful organizations, responsibility does not rest with a single executive or technology team. Instead, governance is coordinated through a cross-functional leadership group that brings together business, technology, legal, security, risk, and compliance perspectives.

This collaborative structure is commonly established through an AI Council, which forms the focus of the next section. Figure 6-2 illustrates how effective governance provides the foundation for responsible AI adoption, creating the clarity and oversight needed as organisations expand their use of AI.

***Figure 6-2.** Governance As the Foundation for Responsible AI*

Building an AI Council

As organizations move beyond isolated AI initiatives, decision-making inevitably becomes more complex.

During the early stages of adoption, many decisions can be made within individual business units. A department may identify a promising use case, evaluate an AI capability, and launch a pilot with support from its technology team. Because the scope is limited, governance is often relatively straightforward.

As AI adoption grows, however, those decisions begin to affect a much wider part of the organization.

A marketing team may want to introduce AI-assisted content creation. Human resources may explore AI for recruitment and employee support. Finance may evaluate AI for forecasting, while customer service teams look to improve response times through AI-powered assistants. Each initiative may appear independent, yet many of the underlying questions are shared.

Should the organization adopt multiple AI platforms or standardize on a common approach?

How should new AI use cases be evaluated?

Who decides whether a proposed solution aligns with organizational priorities?

How should risks, compliance obligations, and Responsible AI principles be assessed before deployment?

Questions such as these cannot usually be answered by a single department.

They require perspectives from across the organization.

This is why many organizations establish an AI Council.

An AI Council is not intended to replace existing governance structures or create additional bureaucracy. Instead, it provides a forum where business and technology leaders can make informed decisions together, ensuring that AI initiatives remain aligned with organizational objectives while maintaining appropriate oversight.

The composition of an AI Council will naturally differ from one organization to another. However, successful councils typically bring together representatives from business leadership, technology, information security, legal, compliance, risk management, data governance, and human resources. Each function contributes a different perspective, helping the organization balance innovation with responsibility.

Consider a proposal to introduce an AI-powered assistant that helps employees answer internal policy questions.

From a business perspective, the initiative may improve productivity and reduce time spent searching for information. Technology teams may evaluate the technical feasibility and integration approach. Security specialists will consider how organizational information is protected. Legal and compliance teams may review regulatory obligations, while human resources may assess how employees will be supported during adoption.

Viewed independently, each perspective is valuable.

Viewed together, they lead to stronger decisions.

This collaborative approach is one of the defining characteristics of successful AI transformation. Rather than allowing individual departments to make isolated decisions, organizations create shared ownership for AI strategy, governance, and adoption.

An AI Council also plays an important role in maintaining consistency as AI initiatives expand.

Without a central governance body, different business units may establish their own standards, select different tools, or interpret organizational policies in different ways. While each decision may appear reasonable in isolation, the organization can gradually develop fragmented approaches that become increasingly difficult to manage.

A well-functioning AI Council helps prevent this fragmentation by providing common direction.

It can establish principles for evaluating new AI opportunities, prioritize investments that align with business strategy, encourage the sharing of successful practices across departments, and ensure that Responsible AI principles remain embedded in organizational decision-making.

Importantly, the Council should not become a bottleneck.

Its role is not to review every prompt, approve every experiment, or slow innovation through excessive oversight. Instead, it should focus on strategic decisions, enterprise standards, governance policies, and the long-term direction of the organization's AI program.

The most effective councils encourage innovation by creating clarity.

When employees understand how AI decisions are made, which governance principles apply, and where responsibility lies, they can innovate with greater confidence because expectations are transparent and consistent across the organization.

For AI Transformation Leaders, establishing an AI Council represents an important shift from managing individual AI projects to managing AI as an enterprise capability. It signals that AI is no longer viewed as an isolated technology initiative but as a strategic organizational asset requiring ongoing leadership and cross-functional collaboration.

Even with strong governance in place, however, successful transformation depends on more than executive oversight.

Policies and governance frameworks may define how AI should be used, but they do not automatically encourage employees to embrace new ways of working. Sustainable adoption requires people who can guide, support, and inspire others throughout the organization.

This is where AI adoption teams and AI Champions become essential, helping to translate governance into everyday practice and enabling AI to become part of the organization's culture rather than simply another technology deployment. Figure 6-3 illustrates how an AI Council brings together cross-functional perspectives to support consistent, balanced, and accountable AI decision-making across the organisation.

Figure 6-3. *An Enterprise AI Council in Action*

Creating Adoption Teams and AI Champions

A well-defined governance framework provides direction, but governance alone does not create adoption.

Policies can establish expectations, leadership can communicate a vision, and an AI Council can provide oversight. Yet none of these activities automatically changes how employees work. Real transformation occurs when people begin using AI confidently as part of their everyday responsibilities.

This is often where organizations encounter their next challenge.

Following a successful pilot, leadership may expect adoption to grow naturally across the business. Employees have seen demonstrations, positive use cases have been shared, and the technology is readily available. Despite this, usage often remains concentrated within a small group of enthusiastic early adopters.

The question then becomes:

Why are some employees embracing AI while others remain hesitant?

The answer is rarely a lack of technology.

More often, employees are uncertain about when AI should be used, how it fits within their existing responsibilities, or whether they can trust the outputs it produces. Some may worry that AI will replace aspects of their role, while others simply lack the confidence to experiment with unfamiliar ways of working.

These concerns are entirely normal.

Throughout the history of workplace technology, successful adoption has depended as much on people as it has on the technology itself. AI is no different.

For this reason, many organizations establish dedicated adoption teams to support the transition from pilot projects to everyday business use.

Unlike governance bodies, which focus on strategy, oversight, and organizational standards, adoption teams concentrate on helping employees succeed with AI. They coordinate communication, organize training activities, gather feedback from business users, identify adoption barriers, and work closely with different departments to ensure that AI is introduced in ways that support existing business processes rather than disrupt them.

Perhaps more importantly, adoption teams help create consistency.

Without coordinated support, different departments may develop their own approaches to AI, resulting in varying levels of confidence, inconsistent practices, and duplicated effort. A dedicated adoption team helps establish a common experience across the organization, making it easier for employees to learn from one another and adopt proven practices.

Alongside formal adoption teams, many organizations also identify AI Champions.

An AI Champion is not necessarily the most technically skilled individual within a department. Instead, they are people who are willing to explore new ways of working, share their experiences, support colleagues, and encourage responsible use of AI within their own teams.

Their influence comes through trust rather than authority.

Employees often feel more comfortable asking questions of a colleague who understands the realities of their day-to-day work than attending another formal presentation or reading additional guidance documents. AI Champions help bridge the gap between organizational strategy and practical implementation by demonstrating how AI can support real business activities.

Consider a finance department introducing Microsoft 365 Copilot.

While central training sessions may explain the product's capabilities, employees are often more interested in practical questions.

- How can AI help prepare monthly reports?
- Can it summarize lengthy financial documents?
- What tasks should still be completed manually?
- What information should never be shared with AI?

These questions are frequently answered most effectively by someone who understands both the technology and the department's daily responsibilities.

This is where AI Champions add considerable value.

Their role extends beyond demonstrating features. They encourage experimentation within agreed governance boundaries, help colleagues develop confidence, identify successful practices worth sharing across the organization, and provide valuable feedback to adoption teams and leadership about the challenges employees continue to face.

Importantly, organizations should avoid viewing AI Champions as permanent owners of AI adoption.

Their purpose is to encourage broader organizational capability rather than becoming the only people who understand AI. Success is achieved when confidence spreads throughout the workforce and AI becomes a normal part of everyday business operations.

For AI Transformation Leaders, this creates an important leadership lesson.

Technology adoption is rarely achieved through executive announcements or software deployment alone. Sustainable adoption develops through continuous engagement, practical support, peer learning, and visible examples of success. When employees see trusted colleagues using AI responsibly to improve their work, confidence grows far more quickly than through formal communications alone.

As adoption expands across the organization, another challenge naturally emerges.

Employees may be willing to use AI, but successful adoption also depends on helping people understand how AI fits within their roles, addressing concerns about change, and developing the knowledge needed to use AI responsibly and effectively.

This brings us to the next aspect of sustainable AI transformation: building AI literacy and managing organizational change. Figure 6-4 illustrates how AI Champions help translate organisational AI strategy into practical adoption by supporting colleagues, sharing experience, and encouraging responsible use within their teams.

Figure 6-4. *How AI Champions Accelerate Organizational Adoption*

Change Management and AI Literacy

Even with effective governance, a committed AI Council, and enthusiastic AI Champions, organizations cannot assume that adoption will happen automatically.

People rarely change the way they work simply because a new technology becomes available.

This has been true for every major technology shift, from email and cloud computing to mobile working and digital collaboration platforms. Artificial intelligence follows the same pattern. While some employees quickly embrace new capabilities, others need time to understand how those capabilities fit within their responsibilities and how they can be used safely and effectively.

This is why successful AI transformation is fundamentally about people as much as it is about technology.

One of the first barriers organizations often encounter is uncertainty.

Employees may recognize that AI has the potential to improve productivity, yet still hesitate to use it in their daily work. They may be unsure when AI is appropriate, whether they can trust its responses, or how its use aligns with organizational policies. Others may worry about making mistakes, exposing sensitive information, or becoming overly dependent on AI for tasks that still require professional judgment.

These concerns should not be dismissed.

In many cases, they reflect a healthy sense of responsibility rather than resistance to innovation.

Leaders who acknowledge these concerns openly are generally more successful than those who assume employees will simply adapt over time. Building confidence begins by creating an environment where people feel comfortable asking questions, experimenting responsibly, and learning from experience without fear of criticism.

This is where AI literacy becomes essential.

AI literacy is not about teaching every employee how large language models work or expecting business users to understand the technical architecture behind generative AI. Instead, it is about developing the practical knowledge needed to use AI confidently, responsibly, and effectively within the context of their own roles.

An employee preparing a presentation, reviewing a policy document, analyzing customer feedback, or drafting a business proposal does not need to become an AI specialist. What they do need is an understanding of when AI can assist, when human judgment remains essential, and how organizational guidance should influence the way AI is used.

As AI literacy improves, confidence often grows alongside it.

Employees begin to recognize that AI is not intended to replace professional expertise but to complement it. Routine activities can often be completed more efficiently, allowing more time for critical thinking, collaboration, creativity, and decision-making. Rather than viewing AI as a substitute for experience, employees begin to see it as another tool that supports better outcomes.

Leadership plays an important role throughout this transition.

Employees pay close attention to how leaders use AI and how they talk about it. If leaders demonstrate responsible use, encourage learning, and openly discuss both the opportunities and limitations of AI, they help establish realistic expectations across the organization. Conversely, if AI is presented as either a threat or a perfect solution to every business challenge, confidence can quickly diminish when reality proves more complex.

Another lesson observed across many AI transformation programs is that communication should continue long after the initial deployment.

Organizations sometimes invest significant effort in announcing new AI capabilities but devote far less attention to supporting employees in the months that follow. Sustainable adoption requires ongoing communication, regular learning opportunities, the sharing of successful business examples, and continuous feedback from employees about the challenges they continue to encounter.

This creates a cycle of continuous improvement.

As employees become more confident, they identify new opportunities for AI. Those experiences generate additional learning, which can then be shared across teams through AI Champions, adoption teams, and leadership communities. Over time, AI becomes less of a separate initiative and more of a natural part of everyday business operations.

For AI Transformation Leaders, perhaps the most important lesson is this:

Technology may introduce change, but people determine whether that change becomes lasting transformation.

Organizations that invest in AI literacy, encourage responsible experimentation, and support employees throughout the adoption journey are far more likely to achieve sustainable business value than those that focus solely on deploying new capabilities.

As organizations mature in their AI journey, attention naturally turns toward another leadership consideration. Widespread adoption brings new commercial questions about licensing models, investment decisions, and ensuring that AI capabilities are aligned with business priorities and long-term value.

These considerations form the focus of the next section on Licensing and Commercial Considerations for Microsoft AI. Figure 6-5 illustrates how effective change management and AI literacy can help remove common barriers to adoption and build employee confidence in using AI responsibly.

***Figure 6-5.** Removing Barriers to AI Adoption*

Licensing and Commercial Considerations for Microsoft AI

Selecting an AI capability is only one part of the decision-making process. Leaders must also consider how that capability will be licensed, funded, and introduced across the organization in a way that supports long-term business objectives.

This is an area where organizations occasionally underestimate the complexity of AI transformation.

During the early stages of experimentation, licensing decisions often appear straightforward. A small pilot may involve only a limited number of users, making costs relatively easy to manage. As AI adoption expands across departments, however, commercial considerations become significantly more important.

Questions begin to emerge.

- Which employees require access to AI capabilities?
- Should every user receive the same level of functionality?
- Would a subscription-based approach provide better value than a consumption-based model?
- How can organizations balance business demand with responsible investment?

These are leadership decisions rather than technical ones.

They require organizations to evaluate expected business value alongside financial considerations, operational priorities, and long-term adoption plans.

One important principle is that different Microsoft AI solutions use different commercial models.

For example, productivity-focused AI experiences, such as Microsoft 365 Copilot, are typically licensed for individual users. Organizations therefore need to consider which roles will benefit most from these capabilities and how adoption can be expanded over time in line with business priorities.

By contrast, many Azure AI services and Microsoft Foundry capabilities follow consumption-based pricing, where costs are influenced by how extensively services are used. This provides organizations with considerable flexibility but also introduces the need for ongoing monitoring, budgeting, and governance as AI usage grows.

Neither approach is inherently better.

Each supports different business scenarios.

Subscription licensing can provide predictable costs for employees who use AI regularly as part of their daily work. Consumption-based services may be more appropriate for custom applications, customer-facing solutions, or workloads where usage naturally fluctuates.

For AI Transformation Leaders, the objective is not to become experts in licensing terminology.

Instead, they should understand that commercial decisions influence adoption strategy.

Providing every employee with the same AI capability may not always represent the most effective investment. Equally, restricting access too heavily may prevent organizations from realizing the broader productivity and innovation benefits that AI can deliver.

Successful organizations therefore align licensing decisions with business objectives rather than technology availability.

Employees whose responsibilities involve creating content, analyzing information, preparing reports, or supporting customers may experience significant productivity improvements through AI-assisted tools. Other roles may require different capabilities or may benefit more from AI embedded within business applications than from individual productivity assistants.

Licensing should therefore reflect how people work rather than assuming that every user has identical needs.

Commercial planning should also extend beyond the initial deployment.

As AI adoption increases, organizations should regularly evaluate whether existing licensing arrangements continue to support business demand. New use cases may emerge, departments may identify additional opportunities, and changing organizational priorities may influence where investment delivers the greatest return.

This reinforces an important leadership principle.

Licensing is not simply a procurement exercise completed at the beginning of an AI program. It is an ongoing strategic decision that should evolve alongside organizational adoption, governance, and business value.

Another consideration is avoiding decisions based solely on cost.

While financial stewardship remains important, selecting the least expensive option does not always produce the greatest organizational benefit. Equally, investing in the most advanced AI capability does not guarantee meaningful business outcomes.

The most effective organizations evaluate licensing decisions in the same way they evaluate AI initiatives themselves: by considering expected value, user needs, governance requirements, and long-term sustainability together rather than in isolation.

For AI Transformation Leaders, licensing should therefore be viewed as an enabler of Responsible AI adoption rather than an administrative task. Well-informed commercial decisions help organizations introduce AI at an appropriate pace, expand adoption where value is demonstrated, and maintain alignment between technology investment and strategic business priorities.

As AI programs mature, leaders also need to understand whether these investments are delivering the intended outcomes. This requires looking beyond deployment numbers or license allocations and instead measuring how AI is influencing productivity, adoption, user confidence, and business performance.

The next section explores how organizations can measure AI success and establish a culture of continuous improvement as AI adoption continues to grow. Figure 6-6 illustrates how licensing and commercial decisions should be aligned with user needs, expected business value, and broader organisational priorities.

Figure 6-6. *Aligning Licensing Decisions with Business Value*

Measuring Success and Continuous Improvement

One of the most encouraging moments in any AI program is seeing employees begin to use the technology in their daily work. Usage increases, new ideas emerge, and different business units identify opportunities to improve the way they operate.

While these are positive signs, they do not necessarily indicate that the organization is achieving meaningful business value.

This distinction is important.

A successful AI transformation should not be measured solely by the number of licenses assigned, prompts submitted, or AI tools deployed. These figures can demonstrate activity, but activity alone does not confirm that the organization is working more effectively or delivering better outcomes.

For leaders, the more important question is not *"How much is AI being used?"* but rather *"What difference is AI making?"*

The answer will vary from one organization to another because every AI initiative is intended to solve a different business problem.

A customer service team may be looking to reduce response times while maintaining service quality. A legal department may want to accelerate document reviews without compromising accuracy. Human resources may focus on reducing administrative effort so that more time can be devoted to employee engagement. Finance teams may seek faster analysis and reporting to support better decision-making.

Although the objectives differ, they all have one characteristic in common.

They define success in terms of business outcomes rather than technology usage.

This is why effective measurement should begin with the objectives established at the start of the initiative.

If the purpose of introducing AI was to improve productivity, leaders should consider whether employees are completing work more efficiently. If the objective was to improve customer experience, attention should focus on customer satisfaction, service quality, and consistency rather than simply the volume of AI interactions. Where AI has been introduced to support better decision-making, organizations should evaluate whether decisions are becoming faster, more informed, or more consistent.

Another important indicator is employee confidence.

Even when AI capabilities are available, employees may avoid using them if they lack trust in the results or remain uncertain about organizational expectations. Regular feedback from business users often provides valuable insight into whether AI is genuinely supporting their work or creating additional effort through unnecessary review and correction.

This highlights an important leadership responsibility.

Measurement should not be viewed as an activity performed only at the end of a project. Instead, it should continue throughout the AI adoption journey, providing leaders with the information needed to refine governance, improve training, address adoption barriers, and identify new opportunities for business value.

Successful organizations also recognize that AI transformation is rarely completed after the first deployment.

- Business priorities change.
- Employees discover new ways of working.
- Technology capabilities continue to evolve.
- Regulatory expectations develop.

Each of these changes presents an opportunity to learn and improve.

Rather than treating AI implementation as a one-time project, leading organizations establish a cycle of continuous improvement. They regularly review outcomes, listen to feedback from employees and customers, evaluate whether governance remains appropriate, and adjust their AI strategy as organizational needs evolve.

This approach creates an environment where learning becomes part of the transformation process.

Early experiences inform future decisions. Successful practices are shared across departments. Challenges identified by one business unit help improve adoption across others. Over time, the organization develops greater confidence not only in the technology but also in its ability to manage AI responsibly and effectively.

For AI Transformation Leaders, perhaps the most valuable measure of success is sustainability.

An AI initiative should continue creating value long after the excitement of the initial deployment has passed. If employees continue to trust the technology, governance evolves alongside changing requirements, and new opportunities for improvement are identified regularly, the organization is far more likely to achieve lasting business benefits.

This perspective also changes the way leaders think about scaling.

Scaling should not simply mean expanding AI to more users or deploying additional solutions. It should mean extending proven practices, maintaining governance, and ensuring that business value continues to grow as adoption increases across the enterprise.

The next section explores how organizations can scale AI responsibly while preserving the trust, governance, and organizational discipline established throughout their transformation journey. Figure 6-7 illustrates why AI success should be evaluated through business outcomes, user confidence, and continuous improvement rather than adoption or usage metrics alone.

Figure 6-7. *Measuring AI Success Beyond Adoption*

Scaling AI Responsibly Across the Enterprise

A successful pilot often creates a sense of momentum within an organization.

Business leaders see encouraging results, employees begin identifying new opportunities, and departments that were not involved in the original initiative become interested in exploring how AI could support their own objectives. From a transformation perspective, this is a positive sign. It demonstrates that AI is beginning to generate confidence beyond its initial use case.

However, this is also the stage where organizations face one of their most important leadership decisions.

Should AI be deployed as quickly as possible across the enterprise, or should growth be managed more deliberately?

Experience suggests that sustainable transformation rarely comes from rapid expansion alone.

Scaling AI successfully is not simply about increasing the number of users, introducing additional AI capabilities, or expanding into more business functions. It is about ensuring that the governance, organizational readiness, and business discipline established during the early stages continue to mature as adoption grows.

This is why scaling should be viewed as an organizational capability rather than a deployment activity.

During the pilot phase, leaders are often closely involved in decisions. Teams work together regularly, governance discussions are manageable, and new use cases receive detailed attention. As AI adoption expands, this level of oversight naturally becomes more difficult.

Different business units begin identifying their own priorities. New AI-enabled processes emerge. Additional information sources become available. Employee expectations evolve, and regulatory requirements may also change over time.

Without a consistent approach, organizations can quickly find themselves managing multiple AI initiatives that operate independently, follow different practices, and deliver varying levels of business value.

Responsible scaling helps avoid this situation.

Rather than encouraging every department to move at its own pace, successful organizations establish common principles that support both innovation and consistency. Governance continues to provide oversight. AI Councils review strategic direction rather than individual projects. Adoption teams share successful practices across business functions, while AI Champions help employees build confidence within their own departments.

The result is that growth becomes coordinated rather than fragmented.

Another characteristic of responsible scaling is recognizing that not every AI opportunity should be pursued immediately.

As enthusiasm for AI increases, organizations often generate far more ideas than they can realistically implement. Attempting to deliver every opportunity at once may stretch resources, create inconsistent user experiences, and make governance increasingly difficult to maintain.

Leaders therefore need to make deliberate choices.

Some initiatives will deliver immediate business value and justify broader investment. Others may require additional preparation, stronger data foundations, or clearer governance before they are ready to move beyond experimentation. Responsible scaling is therefore as much about prioritization as it is about expansion.

An equally important consideration is maintaining organizational trust.

Employees who have developed confidence in AI expect that confidence to remain as new capabilities are introduced. Customers expect their information to continue being handled responsibly. Regulators expect organizations to demonstrate appropriate oversight regardless of how widely AI is adopted.

Scaling should never weaken the governance practices that helped establish trust in the first place.

Instead, governance should evolve alongside adoption, ensuring that new use cases continue to align with organizational policies, Responsible AI principles, and changing business priorities.

Successful organizations also recognize that scaling is not a destination.

As AI capabilities continue to evolve, organizations will encounter new opportunities, new challenges, and new expectations. Governance frameworks will mature. Business priorities will change. Employees will develop new skills, and AI itself will become increasingly integrated into everyday business processes.

For this reason, scaling should be viewed as a continuous journey of learning and adaptation rather than the final stage of an implementation program.

For AI Transformation Leaders, the objective is not simply to expand AI across the enterprise.

The objective is to expand confidence.

When governance remains effective, employees continue to trust the technology, business value is measured consistently, and learning is shared across the organization, AI can evolve from a collection of individual projects into a sustainable organizational capability that supports long-term transformation.

This perspective also brings together the themes explored throughout the chapter.

Governance establishes direction.

AI Councils provide strategic oversight.

Adoption teams and AI Champions encourage confidence.

AI literacy enables responsible use.

Commercial decisions align investment with business priorities.

Continuous improvement ensures that value grows over time.

Together, these elements create the foundation for sustainable enterprise AI transformation.

The next section introduces the SCALE Framework, a practical leadership model that brings these concepts together into a simple approach for evaluating whether an organization is prepared to adopt, govern, and scale AI successfully. Figure 6-8 illustrates how responsible scaling extends AI adoption across the enterprise while maintaining governance, organisational readiness, trust, and business value.

Figure 6-8. *Scaling AI Across the Enterprise*

The SCALE Framework

Throughout this chapter, one message has remained consistent.

Successful AI transformation is not achieved simply by deploying AI technologies. It is achieved by creating an organization that is prepared to adopt AI responsibly, govern it effectively, and expand its use in ways that continue to deliver measurable business value.

Technology enables transformation.

People, governance, and leadership sustain it.

For AI Transformation Leaders, the challenge is often knowing where to focus their attention as AI programs evolve. Organizations must make decisions about governance, encourage adoption, support employees, evaluate commercial investments, and ensure that growth remains aligned with business objectives. Looking at these activities independently can make transformation appear far more complicated than it needs to be.

To bring these ideas together, consider the **SCALE Framework**.

The framework provides a practical leadership lens for evaluating whether an organization is prepared not only to introduce AI but also to sustain and expand its use across the enterprise.

It consists of five interconnected elements: **Strategy Alignment, Council and Governance, Adoption and Champions, Literacy and Learning, and Enterprise Scale.**

S—Strategy Alignment

Every successful AI initiative begins with a clear business purpose.

AI should never be introduced simply because the technology is available or because competitors are investing in it. Organizations achieve the greatest value when AI initiatives directly support strategic objectives such as improving customer experience, increasing productivity, reducing operational complexity, strengthening decision-making, or creating new business opportunities.

Strategy also provides an important mechanism for prioritization.

Most organizations will identify more AI opportunities than they can realistically pursue. Aligning initiatives with organizational priorities helps leaders focus investment where it is most likely to create measurable business value.

C—Council and Governance

Strong governance enables confident innovation.

An AI Council provides cross-functional leadership, ensuring that business, technology, legal, security, compliance, risk management, and operational perspectives are considered together. Rather than approving every individual AI initiative, the Council establishes governance principles, promotes consistent decision-making, and helps ensure that Responsible AI remains embedded throughout the organization.

Effective governance creates clarity.

When employees understand organizational expectations, they are better equipped to innovate responsibly.

A—Adoption and Champions

Technology creates value only when people choose to use it.

Adoption teams help organizations introduce AI consistently by supporting communication, enablement, and user engagement across different business functions. AI Champions complement this effort by encouraging peer learning, sharing practical experience, and helping colleagues develop confidence through everyday use.

Together, they help transform AI from an isolated technology initiative into a capability that employees actively embrace.

L—Literacy and Learning

AI capabilities will continue to evolve.

Consequently, organizations must also continue learning.

AI literacy is not about turning every employee into an AI specialist. It is about helping people understand how to use AI responsibly, recognize its strengths and limitations, and apply professional judgment alongside AI-generated outputs.

Organizations that encourage continuous learning are generally better positioned to adapt as technologies, regulations, and business priorities change over time.

E—Enterprise Scale

Scaling represents the outcome of the previous four elements working together.

Enterprise scale is not measured by the number of AI tools deployed or the number of employees using AI. It is measured by whether AI continues to create business value while maintaining governance, trust, and organizational confidence as adoption expands.

Successful scaling is deliberate.

It builds upon proven practices, reinforces responsible governance, and continuously evaluates outcomes to ensure that AI remains aligned with organizational strategy.

Taken together, the SCALE Framework provides leaders with a practical way to evaluate organizational maturity throughout the AI transformation journey.

It reminds us that sustainable AI success depends on much more than technology. Organizations must align AI with business strategy, establish effective governance, support their workforce, encourage continuous learning, and expand adoption responsibly.

When these five elements evolve together, AI becomes more than a collection of individual projects.

It becomes a trusted organizational capability that supports long-term innovation, resilience, and business growth.

Figure 6-9 brings these five elements together, illustrating how the SCALE Framework helps organizations move from isolated AI initiatives to sustainable enterprise transformation.

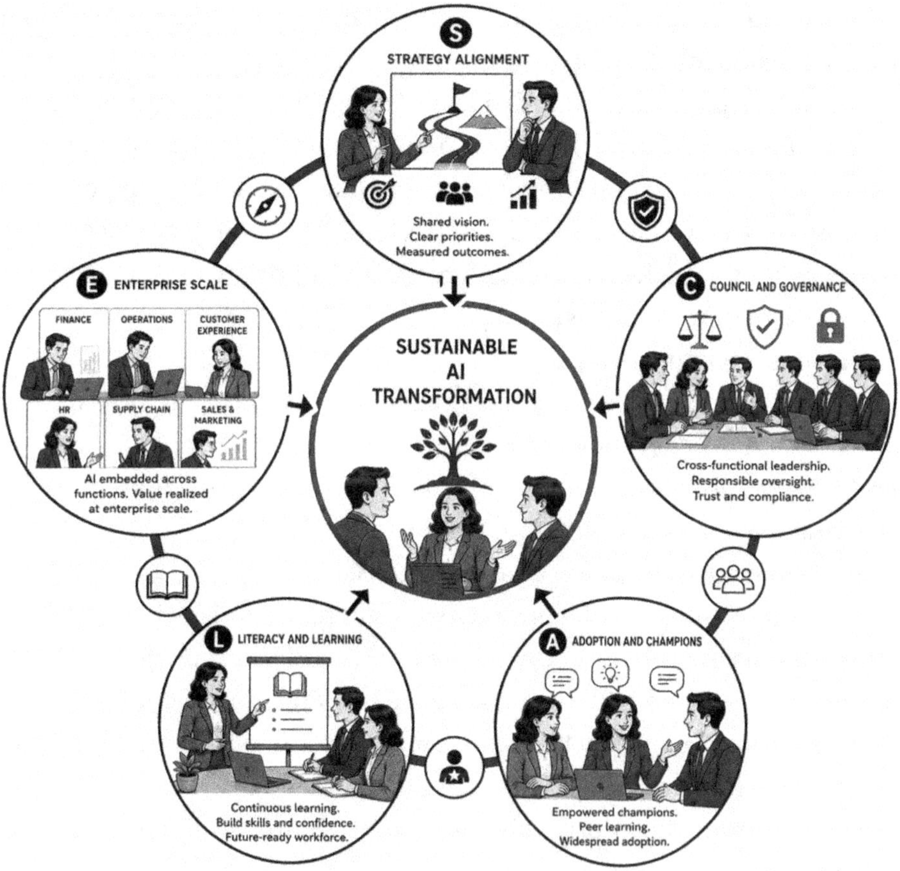

Figure 6-9. *The SCALE Framework for Sustainable AI Transformation*

Leader's Lens

One observation becomes increasingly clear as organizations progress through their AI transformation journey.

The greatest challenges are rarely technical.

Most organizations can identify suitable AI capabilities, establish pilot projects, and demonstrate promising early results. Modern AI platforms are more accessible than ever, and many of the technical barriers that once limited adoption have been significantly reduced.

Yet despite these advances, not every organization succeeds in turning successful pilots into lasting business transformation.

The difference is often found in leadership rather than technology.

Technology can introduce new capabilities, but it cannot establish governance, create organizational trust, encourage collaboration, or help employees embrace new ways of working. These are leadership responsibilities, and they become increasingly important as AI adoption expands across the enterprise.

One pattern appears repeatedly.

When AI initiatives struggle, organizations often respond by searching for better technology. A newer model is evaluated, another platform is introduced, or additional functionality is added in the hope that the next deployment will produce different results.

Occasionally, those changes are appropriate.

More often, however, the underlying challenge lies elsewhere.

Employees may not understand how AI should be used within their roles. Different business units may be working toward conflicting priorities. Governance may be inconsistent across departments. Success may be measured by deployment rather than business outcomes. In these situations, introducing more technology rarely addresses the root cause of the problem.

The organizations that consistently realize value from AI tend to approach transformation differently.

They recognize that adoption is an ongoing organizational capability rather than a single implementation project. They invest in governance before complexity increases. They encourage collaboration between business and technology leaders. They help employees build confidence through continuous learning. Most importantly, they remain focused on the business outcomes that AI is intended to achieve rather than becoming distracted by every new technological advancement.

This perspective also changes how leaders respond to setbacks.

When adoption slows, they ask what barriers employees are experiencing rather than questioning the technology alone.

When governance challenges emerge, they strengthen organizational decision-making instead of introducing additional controls that discourage innovation.

When new AI capabilities become available, they evaluate how those capabilities support business strategy rather than adopting them simply because they are new.

Over time, these organizations develop something that is often more valuable than the technology itself.

They develop organizational confidence.

Employees trust that AI is being introduced responsibly.

Business leaders understand how AI supports strategic priorities.

Governance evolves alongside innovation rather than attempting to catch up with it.

Learning becomes continuous rather than event-driven.

As a result, AI becomes embedded in the way the organization works rather than remaining a series of disconnected technology initiatives.

For AI Transformation Leaders, this may be the most important lesson of all.

Successful AI transformation is not defined by how quickly an organization deploys AI.

It is defined by how effectively the organization enables people, governance, and leadership to evolve alongside the technology.

When those elements grow together, AI becomes more than a productivity tool.

It becomes a sustainable capability that helps the organization adapt, innovate, and create long-term business value.

Exam-Style Questions

Question 1

Your organization has successfully completed an AI pilot within the customer service department. Encouraged by the results, several business units want to introduce their own AI solutions immediately.

As the AI Transformation Leader, what would be the most appropriate next step?

A. Allow each department to select and deploy the AI solution that best suits its own requirements

B. Pause further expansion until a governance approach is established that can support organization-wide adoption

C. Deploy the same AI solution to every department as quickly as possible

D. Delay all future AI initiatives until every employee has completed advanced AI training

Correct Answer

B

Explanation

Successful pilots demonstrate potential, but scaling AI without governance can lead to inconsistent practices, duplicated effort, and increased organizational risk. Establishing governance provides the foundation for sustainable enterprise adoption.

Question 2

During an executive meeting, the Chief Financial Officer, Chief Information Officer, Head of Legal, and Head of Human Resources disagree about approving a new AI initiative. Each raises different concerns based on their area of responsibility.

Which organizational structure is specifically designed to support this type of decision-making?

A. Project Management Office

B. Enterprise Architecture Review Board

C. AI Council

D. Information Security Committee

Correct Answer

C

Explanation

An AI Council brings together cross-functional leadership to balance innovation, governance, legal, security, compliance, and business priorities when making AI-related decisions.

Question 3

An organization has introduced AI across several business units. Six months later, leadership discovers that different departments have adopted different governance practices and conflicting approaches to Responsible AI.

What does this situation most strongly suggest?

A. Employees require more AI licenses

B. Governance has not evolved at the same pace as AI adoption

C. The organization selected the wrong AI model

D. AI should be restricted to technology teams

Correct Answer

B

Explanation

As AI adoption expands, governance must mature alongside it to maintain consistency, accountability, and organizational trust.

Question 4

A newly formed AI adoption team has been asked to support the organization's AI transformation program.

Which activity would best demonstrate the team's primary purpose?

A. Developing new AI foundation models

B. Helping employees adopt AI confidently through communication, enablement, and ongoing support

C. Approving all AI purchases across the organization

D. Managing the organization's cloud infrastructure

Correct Answer

B

Explanation

Adoption teams focus on helping employees integrate AI into everyday work by supporting communication, training, and organizational change.

Question 5

One department consistently reports higher AI adoption than the rest of the organization. Leadership discovers that a respected employee regularly demonstrates practical AI use cases, answers colleagues' questions, and encourages responsible experimentation.

Which concept best explains this success?

A. AI governance

B. AI Champion

C. Licensing optimization

D. Technical architecture

Correct Answer

B

Explanation

AI Champions build confidence through peer learning and practical support, helping colleagues adopt AI within their own business context.

Question 6

Several employees have access to AI tools but rarely use them. When asked why, they explain that they are unsure when AI should be used and are concerned about making mistakes.

What should leadership prioritize?

A. Purchasing additional AI licenses

B. Replacing the existing AI platform

C. Strengthening AI literacy and organizational support

D. Restricting AI access until confidence improves

Correct Answer

C

Explanation

Hesitation is often addressed through education, guidance, and practical support rather than additional technology.

Question 7

An executive sponsor asks whether every employee should receive the same Microsoft AI capability from the start of the program.

Which response best reflects a leadership approach to licensing?

A. Every employee should receive identical AI capabilities regardless of business need

B. Licensing decisions should align with user roles, expected business value, and organizational priorities

C. The least expensive licensing option should always be selected

D. Licensing should only be reviewed after the first year of adoption

Correct Answer

B

Explanation

Licensing is a strategic decision that should support business objectives rather than treating every user or workload identically.

Question 8

A year after introducing AI, leadership reports excellent license utilization but struggles to demonstrate measurable business benefits.

Which question should the AI Transformation Leader ask next?

A. Can we purchase more AI licenses?

B. Should we migrate to another AI platform?

C. What measurable business outcomes has AI improved for employees, customers, or the organization?

D. Have all employees submitted enough prompts?

Correct Answer

C

Explanation

Technology usage is only one indicator. AI success should ultimately be measured through business outcomes, productivity, customer value, and organizational impact.

Question 9

A business unit proposes rolling out AI to every department within a single month because the initial pilot was highly successful.

What would be the most appropriate leadership response?

A. Expand immediately while delaying governance until later

B. Scale AI in a planned manner, ensuring governance, adoption, and organizational readiness mature together

C. Limit AI permanently to the original pilot team

D. Focus only on deploying more AI capabilities

Correct Answer

B

Explanation

Responsible scaling balances innovation with governance, workforce readiness, and sustainable business value.

Question 10

At the conclusion of an AI transformation program review, the executive team asks a simple question:

"How do we know whether we're truly ready to scale AI across the enterprise?"

Which response best reflects the **SCALE Framework** introduced in this chapter?

A. Verify that every department is using the same AI tool

B. Confirm that the organization has the largest possible AI budget

C. Evaluate whether AI initiatives align with business strategy, governance is established, employees are adopting AI confidently, continuous learning is encouraged, and the organization is prepared to scale responsibly

D. Measure only the number of AI licenses assigned across the organization

Correct Answer

C

Explanation

The SCALE Framework reminds leaders that sustainable AI transformation depends on **Strategy Alignment, Council and Governance, Adoption and Champions, Literacy and Learning, and Enterprise Scale** working together. Technology alone is never enough.

Final Thoughts

Congratulations on reaching the end of this book. Figure 6-10 captures the final message of this book: AI transformation is ultimately a leadership journey, shaped by responsible decisions, organisational confidence, and the ability to turn AI into lasting business value.

***Figure 6-10.** Final Thoughts by Kasam Shaikh*

If you've read every chapter, I hope you've noticed that this was never intended to be just another certification guide.

My goal wasn't simply to help you answer exam questions. It was to help you think like an AI Transformation Leader.

Technology will continue to evolve. New AI models will emerge, Microsoft will introduce new capabilities, and organizations will discover new ways of applying AI. While those technologies will inevitably change, the leadership principles behind successful AI transformation remain remarkably consistent.

Throughout this book, we've explored that journey together—from understanding the role of an AI Transformation Leader to recognizing business value, applying Responsible AI principles, selecting the right Microsoft AI capabilities, preparing organizations through enterprise readiness, and finally adopting, governing, and scaling AI responsibly.

If there is one message I hope you take away, it is this:

Successful AI transformation is not measured by how much AI an organization deploys. It is measured by the business value it creates, the trust it builds, and the leadership that guides it.

Although this book has been written to support the **Microsoft AB-731: AI Transformation Leader** certification, remember that certification exams evolve over time. Microsoft regularly updates learning content, assessment objectives, and product capabilities to reflect the latest developments.

For that reason, I strongly encourage you to review the **official Microsoft Learn study guide** and any related learning resources before scheduling your exam. The content in this book is aligned with the published exam objectives and Microsoft guidance available at the time of writing, but the official study guide should always be your final reference for the most up-to-date syllabus.

Most importantly, I hope this book has helped you build confidence—not only to pass the exam but also to have meaningful conversations about AI within your organization and make better leadership decisions as AI continues to evolve.

If this book helped you understand the concepts, gave you more confidence, or even played a small part in helping you pass the AB-731 exam, I'd genuinely love to hear from you.

Feel free to connect with me on **LinkedIn** or **X** and let me know how your certification journey went. Hearing from readers is one of the most rewarding parts of writing, and your feedback also helps me improve future editions and create better learning resources for the community.

Finally, thank you for choosing to spend your time with this book. I truly appreciate your trust, and I hope it has been a worthwhile companion on your AI transformation journey.

I wish you every success in your Microsoft AB-731 certification and, more importantly, in applying these principles to create responsible, sustainable, and impactful AI transformation within your organization.

Best of luck with your exam, and I look forward to hearing your success story.

—Kasam Shaikh

Index

A

K. Shaikh, *Microsoft Certified: AI Transformation Leader Study Companion*, Certification Study Companion Series, https://doi.org/10.1007/979-8-8688-3168-3

D

E

F

G

H, I, J, K

L

M, N

O

P, Q

R

S

T, U, V, W, X, Y, Z

GPSR Compliance
The European Union's (EU) General Product Safety Regulation (GPSR) is a set of rules that requires consumer products to be safe and our obligations to ensure this.

If you have any concerns about our products, you can contact us on

ProductSafety@springernature.com

In case Publisher is established outside the EU, the EU authorized representative is:

Springer Nature Customer Service Center GmbH
Europaplatz 3
69115 Heidelberg, Germany

www.ingramcontent.com/pod-product-compliance
Lightning Source LLC
LaVergne TN
LVHW052303200926
848481LV00002B/451

9798868831676